THE
Archive Photographs
SERIES

BISHOPSWORTH
WITHYWOOD AND HARTCLIFFE

Probably Bishopsworth's oldest photograph, this shows Richard Lansdown and his wife Mary, about 1860, though their clothes reflect the fashions of twenty years earlier. Richard may have been the son of William Lansdown, bailiff (1789-1830) at Inn's Court Farm (see p. 16), whose account book along with this splendid framed photograph is preserved in the Bristol Record Office (24759 (14)a). In the 1871 census return, Richard Lansdown is recorded as a labourer at Headley Farm. His wife and daughter, Sarah Lansdown, were laundresses, and his granddaughter, Emily, aged 6, was described as 'scholar', and probably attended Bishopsworth School.

THE Archive Photographs SERIES

BISHOPSWORTH
WITHYWOOD AND HARTCLIFFE

Compiled by
Anton Bantock
and
members of the Malago Society

The MALAGO Society

CHALFORD

First published 1996
Copyright © Anton Bantock
and members of the Malago Society, 1996

The Chalford Publishing Company
St Mary's Mill, Chalford,
Stroud, Gloucestershire, GL6 8NX

ISBN 0 7524 0689 2

Typesetting and origination by
The Chalford Publishing Company
Printed in Great Britain by
Redwood Books, Trowbridge

Front cover illustration:
St Peter's Garden Fête, c. 1934, opened by Sir Ernest Cook (centre) who stands next to the vicar, Revd Langley-Webb. Lady Cook wears a big hat with a striped ribbon. Other notable villagers present were – top, from left to right: James Clark, Mr Pobjoy and Cecil Hill, and on the same row Mrs Jessie Clark in glasses, Mrs Nutt. Behind them, from left to right: Dennis Russell, Anthony Hall and Mr Laws (white hair). Behind the vicar's left shoulder is W.J. Kew and next to him, a little further forward, Mrs Bishop. Back row centre: Alice Gill, with flaming white hair, the village sextoness. Behind W.J. Kew, in a large hat, is Dorothy Hall and her uncle Edwin Wyatt. His caretaker, Agnes Millear, is extreme right in a cloche hat. Except for the little boy, Phillip Gallop, in the back row standing next to father, Charlie, we are unable to identify most of the children. We must not forget the pretty woman in the back row in the large floppy hat; she is Rosa Lovell.

Contents

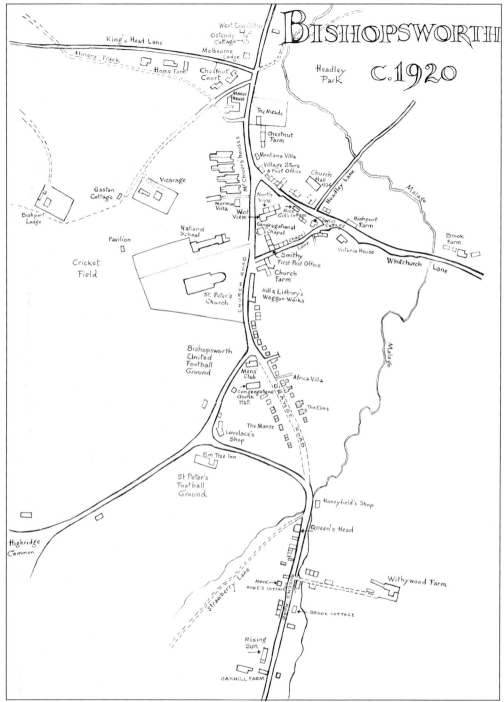

Map of Bishopsworth Village, c. 1920, showing the main buildings and places referred to in this book.

Introduction

Bishopsworth began as a Saxon hamlet on a Roman road and on the highest point of navigation on the Malago. In Saxon times this was a much wider waterway than it is now and was an important communications route. A Saxon hall stood on the site of the Manor House, a place of continuous human occupation for over a thousand years. The Manor of Bishopsworth is mentioned in the Domesday Book and the lands attached to it included all of present-day Hartcliffe, Withywood, Highridge and part of Knowle West. From the twelfth to the sixteenth centuries the Arthur family were Lords of the Manor and in 1190 Robert Arthur gave land for the first church, a chapel of ease constructed on the village triangle – the site now occupied by Bishopsworth Swimming Pool.

Manorial rights declined after the fifteenth century; the Chapel of Ease closed c. 1540 and after 1570 the Arthur family were replaced by absentee landlords – the Smyths of Ashton Court. It was they who rebuilt the Manor House as a dower house c. 1700. Manorial land was progressively taken over by yeoman farmers, although the majority of the farms continued to belong to the Smyths of Ashton Court or the Gore-Langton-Temples of Newton Park.

The period covered by the photographs in this book witnessed the most profound changes to affect the village in all its long history – the transformation from a remote farming community into a bustling suburb of Greater Bristol. In 1843 Bishport, as the village had been vulgarly called for some generations, was a scattered community of 1,050 farmers, field labourers, coal-miners and milk sellers. There was no resident gentry, no resident clergyman until 1853; and, after construction of the new turnpike road to Wells via Pensford and Temple Cloud, the old Wells Road through Bishopsworth was no longer used. The first photographs show a tiny hamlet lost in timeless oblivion and surrounded by vestigial remains of the old forest of Filwood. Situated in the greater valley of the Malago, it was cut off from the city by Bedminster Down – a mile of open heathland and scattered miners' cottages. Until 1922, there was no public transport and, after leaving the tram at the Miners' Arms, villagers climbed the hill on foot, with no streetlights to guide them, and approached the village by an unmetalled road lined with wild hawthorn trees.

The first major changes were the coming of the first Congregational Chapel in 1828, the School in 1842 and St Peter's Church in 1843. The three big houses in the lower village – the Manor House, Chestnut Court and The Meade – were not at that time the nucleus of the community. The gentlemen farmers, who are brilliantly represented in these photographs, were the village aristocracy; they were leaders of society, pillars of church and chapel, members of the Turnpike Trust and the School Boards, and Guardians of the Poor; their tennis and bridge parties were the main form of entertainment. Most of them were related by marriage and functioned like a private club.

The country people worked as labourers or coal-miners, often walking long distances to Pensford or South Liberty Lane in Ashton Vale, or uprooting their whole families and moving to the South Wales collieries when times were bad. Women ran cottage laundries, collecting on foot the dirty linen from the big houses in Clifton, washing and ironing it in unbelievably primitive conditions and returning it for a few shillings a week.

There always existed a degree of mutual suspicion between the upper and lower village. The upper village in Queen's Road (now Withywood) regarded the lower village – the church, the chapel, the big houses, as 'snobbish' and considered Holy Communion at St Peter's to be a 'gentry only' service; while the lower village referred to the pubs and miners' cottages in Queen's Road as 'The Barracks', 'Little Hell' and definitely not nice.

By the end of the nineteenth century, a few professional people had taken up residence in the village; and the building of Edwardian mansions by Mr Walter Chivers, opposite the post office, and by Mr Bishop in Grange Road could have transformed the village into another Knowle or Henleaze had not the First World War intervened. This was only a reprieve, however, as the building of the estates on Bedminster Down after 1928 and Headley Park (1934-38) brought an influx of newcomers which threatened the identity of the village and brought the city boundary to its doorstep. The sale of the Smyth farms in 1917 and the Temple farms in 1924 brought their tenants a release from the landlord system, only for them to be served with compulsory purchase orders by the City of Bristol after 1939 for the construction of new estates up to Dundry Hill.

The Bishopsworth Parish Council, first elected in 1898, maintained a sturdy and independent existence and initiated many improvements – mains water, telephones, drains, public transport; metalled roads arrived by 1930.

The extension of the city boundary in 1951, detaching Bishopsworth from Somerset, and the construction of the Hartcliffe, Highridge and Withywood estates after 1955 engulfed the village. One by one the farms disappeared and their lands were 'developed'. The village triangle and almost all the old cottages in Whitchurch Lane were demolished for road widening around 1960, and Queen's Road was transformed when three-storey maisonettes and shops took the place of labourers' cottages. Surprisingly, Bishopsworth did not lose its identity. The brilliant restoration of the Manor House (1976-80) by Denis Bristow was a catalytic event and stimulated a new desire to preserve the best of the past.

St Peter's Church, the Royal British Legion, the Public Library, the Sartan Club and the Manor House continue to be the focus of the community; people still talk of 'going down to the village'. The upper village still preserves a large proportion of vernacular buildings; and events like the annual Bishopsworth Quiz continue to bring the whole community together. The Malago Society is working to record and make available its history and Malago Valley Conservation Group acts to conserve its heritage and improve its future. The production of this 'album' of photographs has crystallised these activities, resulting in a tangible record for posterity.

This book is mostly about the people who shaped our community. It is dedicated to them and their descendants.

The pictures are arranged largely in chronological order and are grouped by theme. There are no formal chapter breaks; the contents on page 5, however, give a broad indication of how the story of Bishopsworth progresses through the book.

Further Reading

Much of Bishopsworth's history has been published by the Malago Society in *Malago* Magazine and in some special numbers on individual subjects or personalities. Cross references to these have been included in square brackets after the captions using the following abbreviations: M.x – *Malago* Magazine number x; SP – *St Peter's Bishopsworth 1843-1993*; MMW1 – *Mark – My Words*; MMW2 – *Mark: More of My Words*. Much more unpublished material on old Bishopsworth and district exists in the Malago Archives. The pictures come from the extensive photographic archives accumulated and catalogued by the Malago Society. Access to the archives and photographs is by application to the Society via Bishopsworth Library.

Acknowledgements

The Malago Society would like to thank all those who have contributed to this telling of the story of Bishopsworth, whether by working on the book, supplying photographs over the years, mining the archives or recalling their own experiences and those of their families and friends.

The Bishopsworth Story

Approach to Bishopsworth, some time before 1914, looking down Gifford's Hill to Church Road. Not a building in sight, but they are there behind the trees: The Meade on the left, Chestnut Court and the Manor House on the right. A signpost pointing up King's Head Lane reads 'BRIDGWATER ROAD 1 MILE'. On the left, where Bishopsworth Library now stands, was a patch where male paupers were paid 2/6d to break stones to mend the road. In the trap, drawn by a pony called Toby, are Mr Derham, a travelling salesman, and Joe Simmons, later killed in the First World War (see p. 68). At the bottom of the hill is the paper-man with a club foot who delivered newspapers from Bedminster.

Bishopsworth Manor House, then known as Bishport House, before 1890. It was last reconstructed *c.* 1700 by the Smyths of Ashton Court on approximately the same site where the manor and village began, probably in the sixth century. By 1890 it had lost its land, its status and its name and was soon to lose its original early Georgian sash-bars. Following a brilliant restoration (1976-1980) it now closely resembles its late seventeenth century appearance. [M4, M7, M15, M29, M30, M31].

'Home Ground', a field then belonging to Home Farm, now King's Head Park, c. 1890. Along the bottom of this field ran a dirt drive leading to the old Vicarage. It is now Vicarage Road. Through a screen of giant elms can just be seen the rear quarters of the Manor House. Arthur and Lizzie Wyatt of Home Farm (see p. 44) are playing tennis with (right) Blanche Millear, teacher at the National School, and (extreme right) their niece, Clare Britton. On the extreme left is her sister, Nell Britton (p. 35).

Church Road *c.* 1911 was little more than a dirt track, as marks of carriage wheels are clearly visible. On the left is the wall of the Manor House garden and beyond is the entrance to Chestnut Court. The low wall on the right was a favourite spot for courting couples. At this point a culvert under the road carried a tributary of the Malago. On the right side of Gifford's Hill, in the distance, the door of Prospect Cottage is just visible through the branches.

Postcard of the Manor House *c.* 1905, ivy-covered and shorn of its Georgian sash-bars, probably by Walter Chivers who installed his family here in 1901 and made many structural alterations.

Benjamin Hall of Filwood Farm, where the family had lived since at least the seventeenth century, and where Dorothy Hall had sheltered Cavalier fugitives from the Second Siege of Bristol in 1645. At one time Filwood Farm employed nine men and five house servants. [M20, M21, M22, M23].

In 1846 Ben Hall married Elizabeth Winter from Puriton. These are studio photographs of the early 1860s when Elizabeth wore an elaborate crinoline, then in fashion, and the frilly lace cap always worn indoors at that period. She had a lady's maid, Elizabeth Baker, and a governess, Ann Harding, for her five children.

Benjamin Hall's sister, Elizabeth, shown here (left), married his wife's brother, Abraham Winter. She was a woman of great independence and spirit who wrote letters all in verse, raised money for the monument on the battlefield of Sedgemoor and invited herself to Westminster Abbey for the funeral of Queen Victoria. Right: George Winter, brother of Elizabeth Winter, came to Filwood in 1851 with the intention of wooing Benjamin's sister, Maria. He was a great entertainer who wrote verses and narrated them in 'Zummerset' dialect. His party piece, 'To the Coronation', related his misadventures when he travelled up to London for the coronation of Queen Victoria in 1837.

Ann Harding, governess to the Hall children. When Ben and Elizabeth and their youngest son, Abraham, all died in 1864 of diphtheria, Miss Harding took over the management of the farm and brought up the children until they came of age.

Home Farm, *c.* 1890. The house survives relatively unchanged on the edge of King's Head Park, though most of the out-buildings have gone. [M12].

The Wyatt family at Home Farm, *c.* 1864. The heads of John and Joseph have been inserted as neither was at home when the photograph was taken. Mrs Martha Wyatt stands behind the farmer, Joseph. The children are, from left to right: Benjamin, Arthur, John, Edward, Martha (daughter), Joseph (son), Edwin, Sarah. Seated in front: Sidney and Clara. Arthur was the clown of the family and kept them in fits of laughter with his endless high spirits and impromptu songs.

Home Farm House, *c.* 1890. Clara Wyatt is on the left. The miners' track from Bishopsworth to the South Liberty Lane Colliery ran in front of the house and up over Bedminster Down. The sounds of the miners' wooden clogs were as regular as clockwork and the children often threw them turnips to feed the pit ponies.

'When a good innocent child of twelve', wrote Clara Wyatt under this studio portrait of herself and her mother. She was sent as a weekly boarder to a private school in Clifton by her elder brother, Joseph, who was a missionary in India. He wrote to her: 'There is a very large stock of good poetry which you ought to read, for example Tennyson's 'Maude' and 'In Memoriam' and also 'The Princess'. You might, I think, borrow all these books from Mrs Randall.' Clara replied, 'I am getting on pretty well at school, and also with my music. I am learning to play and sing, *O Willie we have missed you.*

Inn's Court Farm, seen here in a watercolour of 1789, was the remnant of a castellated and semi-fortified fifteenth century mansion called Inyn's Court. It was built by Sir John Inyn who fought at Agincourt in 1416, became Judge and Recorder of Bristol and finally Chief Justice and Baron of the Exchequer to Henry VI. He was granted a large estate which became the second manor of Bishopsworth, comprising most of what is now Knowle West and Inns Court. There is a fine brass of Sir John in the Lady Chapel of St Mary Redcliffe.

Only half of one of the original towers of Inyn's Court survived into the twentieth century. In the 1930s, it was being used as a hen house and on one celebrated occasion it was used to lock up a poacher. Threatened with demolition, a campaign was launched in 1952 to save it and now it is incorporated into the Vicarage of the Church of the Holy Cross, Knowle West.

George Flower of Pensford rented Inn's Court farm in 1887 and became a champion dairy farmer and horse dealer. He also acquired Crox Bottom Farm. When he died aged 48, of a clot on the brain, his son Thomas took over and eventually bought Inn's Court Farm, and two other sons, Albert Abraham and Wellington, took on Crox Bottom. [M12].

Rosina Flower, wife of George, c. 1864. She spent her last years at Crox Bottom which she managed so well that she carried off all the prizes offered by the Ashton Court Estate. She was befriended by Dame Emily Smyth who frequently visited the farm and presented Rosina with a modern bathroom, decorated with flowers in virtue of her picturesque name – a marked luxury in farmhouses of that period.

The first church in Bishopsworth was a chapel of ease, founded in 1190. The deed between Arthur, Lord of the Manor, who granted the land, and George of Dunster, Vicar of St John's Bedminster, who conducted the services, still exists in the Bristol Record Office. The chapel was closed and converted into cottages in the 1540s. The 'Old Chappelle Cottages', still bearing traces of medieval wall paintings, survived until 1960 when they were bulldozed for the building of Bishopsworth Swimming Pool.

The stable door in the end cottage was the entrance to Bishopsworth's first post office, c. 1860. The first postmaster was Benjamin Bellamy who doubled up as the blacksmith in the smithy that adjoined his shop in Chapel Lane. This photograph shows the smithy after the arches had been filled in to convert the building into dwellings. It was a favourite trick of Bishopsworth lads to prop up a water butt and lean it against the door of one of these cottages. When they knocked on the door and ran, the poor woman who opened it was drenched with water and her kitchen flooded.

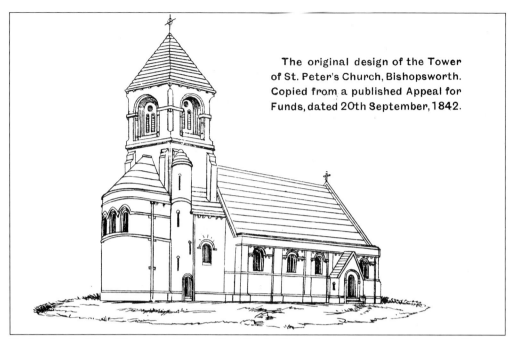

The original design of the Tower of St. Peter's Church, Bishopsworth. Copied from a published Appeal for Funds, dated 20th September, 1842.

Design for the 'New Church at Bishport' by Charles Fripp. It was designed in the mock Norman style with a semi-circular apse and modelled on a Romanesque church at Thaen near Caen in Normandy. Until 1843, Bishopsworth had been in the parish of St John's, Bedminster, and the initiative for creating a new parish came from the Revd W.W. Malet, curate of St John's and Mr W. Goulston, churchwarden, coal owner and principal of the Bedminster Boys' Academy in North Street. [SP].

Water-colour of St Peter's soon after the consecration by the Bishop of Salisbury on 22 April 1843. The absence of wealthy patrons in the locality meant that the £1,500 required for construction fell short of the total by £300, and the tall belfry was never built.

First photograph of St Peter's Church, *c.* 1900, from the Men's Club at the junction of Church Road and Grange Road. There were no houses in sight, many trees, a narrow unmetalled road and a muddy footpath with grass verge.

St Peter's Church, *c.* 1930. The ivy and cypress trees have since disappeared, so have raised pavements which date from the time when roads in winter were more like rivers.

The Church choir, on the steps of the old Vicarage, *c.* 1861. Headed by the vicar, the Revd Goldeney-Randall, and the curate, Edmund Price, were the pillars of the church: Mr Thomas Maynard of The Meade, who was churchwarden; Charles Dallimore Hill, the village grocer; Alfred Froud of Castle Farm; and four Wyatt brothers, including Edwin, who was still singing in the choir 88 years later!

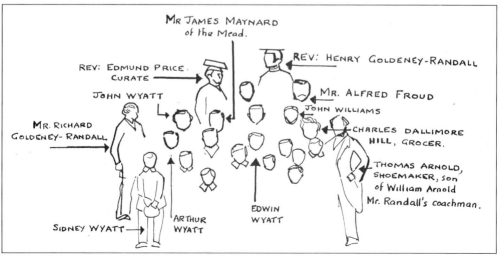

The Revd Henry Goldeney-Randall was the first resident clergyman (1853-1863). The Vicarage was built in 1858 to accommodate his large family and a full complement of servants, including cook, coachman and housemaid. He was a churchman of outstanding zeal and moral rectitude. His unbounded dedication to improve the lot of the villagers led to the rebuilding of the National School and the foundation of a mission at the foot of Bedminster Down where he found the poor mining community 'living in ignorance and neglect of all religion'. This ultimately led to the formation of the separate parish of St Dunstan's. He later became Vicar of St Mary Redcliffe and Archdeacon of Bristol.

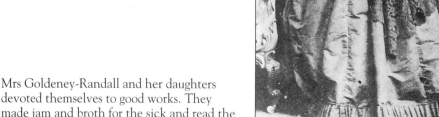

Mrs Goldeney-Randall and her daughters devoted themselves to good works. They made jam and broth for the sick and read the Bible to children in the National School.

Miss Agnes (left) and Miss Gertrude Goldeney-Randall, the vicar's daughters. Their sister Mary died aged eight in 1855 and a window in the church is dedicated to her memory. Gertrude died in 1875 and Agnes in 1878. The cause of their early deaths was almost certainly consumption (TB).

Left: Richard Goldeney-Randall, the vicar's only son, went to Oxford and later became a successful barrister. Right: the Revd Edmund Price was curate, as was the Revd Francis Potts, to whose memory there is a stained-glass window. He was the author of many hymns including *Angel Voices ever Singing*.

The Revd Walter Molesworth, Bishopsworth's longest-serving vicar (1868-1909). A man of unbending principles, he could be ruthless in hounding non-conformist and disobedient choirboys, secular school boards or local farmers who blocked rights of way. Yet his Christianity extended to the material as well as the spiritual needs of his flock as he provided the poor with clothes, winter fuel and established a dispensary in the Vicarage for those who could afford neither doctor nor medicine. 'He always had something in his pocket for us kids,' said one of his parishioners.

The Vicarage in the time of Mr Molesworth. He was a bachelor, and domestic cares were entrusted to a housekeeper, Miss Harriet Church from Painswick. In those days there was an uninterrupted view from the Vicarage windows across Cobhorn to the Church and Dundry Hill. In the garden grew a magnificent ilex tree, which gives the name to Ilex Close, carved out of the Vicarage garden in the 1950s. [SP].

Harry Biddell and his brother, orphans from Painswick, brought up by Mr Molesworth in the Vicarage.

John Maynard Froud, who came to live at the Vicarage with his mother, Louisa, when his father, Israel, an agent on the Ashton Court Estate, succumbed to alcohol. He was the second son of George Froud of Castle Farm (see p. 48). John Maynard Froud later founded a well-known firm of architects. When Mr Molesworth retired in 1904 following a stroke, the church clock was given in his memory and later Molesworth Drive was named after him.

Charles Dallimore Hill was Bishopsworth's first grocer, c. 1860. His father was a Bedminster printer and his grandfather, Peter Dallimore, was a cooper and landlord of The Red Cow in West Street. His shop may well have been the one that was acquired by Mr Lloyd c. 1890 and subsequently by Bernard Clark. Charles and his sons sang in the church choir and all his daughters chose careers rather than husbands.

Kate Hill, one of Mr Charles Hill's daughters, c. 1875. She became a teacher and ran a private school in Brislington. Her sister, Lydia, entered an Anglican Order in the East End of London and her missionary work among the poor took her into parts where even policemen feared to tread. Maggie, another sister, pioneered the teaching of domestic science.

The village shop in the time of Charles Dallimore Hill. The main part of the building is just out of the picture to the left. The part which is visible later served as Bishopsworth's second post office. The cottages at the entrance to Whitchurch Lane survived until the early 1960s when the road was widened to provide the first access to Hartcliffe. To the right is the garden wall of North View, where Mr Froud ran the first village bakery.

Hester Bolt, poor widow and village personality, lived in Gaston Cottage across the fields from Home Farm. In census returns she is variously described a 'pauper' (1851), 'nurse' (1861) and 'laundress' (1871), in which year she appears to have had a ten-year old servant, Elizabeth Derrick. None of these descriptions exactly fits the very grand backdrop in the photographer's studio on Bristol Bridge, where this portrait was taken in 1875, an event almost certainly organised by her neighbours, the Wyatts, to whom she brought lilies of the valley every Whitsuntide from her garden to go into their buttonholes. The cottage still stands, much modernised, and now called 'Ponderosa' (Vicarage Road).

The Meade. A fine Queen Anne style house and a building of some distinction which used to stand opposite the Manor House. For most of the nineteenth century it belonged to the Maynard family. Thomas Maynard (d. 1874) was churchwarden and headed the list of donations to the church building and restoration funds. He placed windows in the chancel in his parents' memory, sang in the choir and was district enumerator in the census.

Thomas Maynard's son, also Thomas, died suddenly, aged 41, in September 1881 on the day of the harvest festival, and the font was donated in his memory. His widow, who had two little girls, Maud and Dolly, later married Tim Davies, shown here, who was an upholster from Stokes Croft. Some say he was a rogue and the family left the village soon afterwards.

View of The Meade in the 1950s. After the Maynards it was the home of Miss Olive Smith and subsequently became the home of Dr Noel Delaney and later his partner, Dr Oliver Jones, who both used part of the house as a surgery. It was demolished c. 1964 for road widening and the new chapel of the Plymouth Brethren took its place.

Chestnut Court, built in 1760 by Joseph Whippie, a gentleman from Whitchurch. By 1858, it was the home of Israel Maynard, cousin of Thomas. When he died, unmarried, in 1880, it passed to a distant cousin, Mrs Maynard-Turner, a 'lady' who put it up for auction in 1888. Edwin Wyatt of Home Farm bid £1,150 and got it. Mrs Maynard-Turner was horrified, exclaiming: 'What, that man Edwin?'. With Chestnut Court, Edwin inherited Mrs Maynard-Turner's impoverished step-son; 'Three pounds would relieve the most pressing need,' wrote the young man from Bury St Edmunds.

Mr Walter Theodore Chivers bought 'Bishport House' in 1902. He was a successful builder and sanitary engineer from Victor Road, West Street, Bedminster. The wedding of Nelly, one of his eight daughters, to Leonard Courtney in 1919 was a great event in the history of the 'Manor House' as it came to be called in his time. Walter and his wife Emily sit on the front row to the right. Also in the picture are their other seven daughters with Norah, who was bridesmaid, in the front row. In the middle row, dressed in white, from left to right: Marie, Mable (next to her husband, Bert Broad) and all together at the end: Millie, Effie and Elsie, with her son Brian. At the end of the back row (right) is Gladys. The Revd Jupp, standing next to his wife, was vicar at the time. [M30, M31].

Mabel, the third eldest, married Bert Broad, dairy farmer of White House Farm (now part of Hartcliffe). She was the longest surviving member of the family and died aged 102 in 1990.

Joseph Henry Mitchell who married the second daughter, Elsie Chivers. They lived in Oak Villa, Grange Road, and had two sons, Brian and Colin, and a daughter, Denise. Before her marriage, Elsie was a telephonist and won a commendation for being one the fastest switchboard operators in Bristol.

Three of Walter Chivers' daughters. From left to right: Norah (no. 7) with Bert Shaler, Millie (no. 1) and Effie (no. 8). There were no servants at the Manor House and the Chivers' daughters were brought up to be self-sufficient and independent. Three of them never married and continued to live at the Manor House until 1949, three years after the death of their father.

Filwood Farm, a building of great antiquity, with buttressed walls and mullioned windows, may have been a medieval hunting lodge of the Royal Forest of Filwood and possibly Manor House of the last village of Fylton (or Philton). In the sitting room was a cavernous fireplace up which a holly bush was dragged on a length of rope each year to remove the soot, and on the walls hung two shotguns, a sword and a rapier. The farm belonged to Lord Temple's estate but had been worked by the Hall family for hundreds of years and was finally bought by them in 1924. [M6, M7, M8].

In 1886 Benjamin Hall, farmer of Filwood, eldest son of Benjamin Hall and Elizabeth Winter (see p. 12) married Clara Wyatt of Home Farm (see p. 15). This delightfully natural photograph c. 1905 shows Ben and Clara with their children: Win and Dorothy standing, Sidney in Norfolk jacket, Anthony with the sun in his eyes and baby, Phyllis, who died aged eight of peritonitis. Sidney was killed at Gallipoli in 1915 and Dorothy lived until 1987. She was the inspiration behind the Malago Society and the source of many of these photos and anecdotes.

Joe Bellamy, cowman at Filwood Farm, *c.* 1910. He lived in a cottage in Whitchurch Lane and walked every day to Filwood to round up the cows for milking before 6.00 a.m. He then went into the kitchen to eat his breakfast – a mug of tea and a 'doorstep' cut from a cottage loaf into which he put a bit of bacon and mustard. Young Sidney Hall was so fascinated by this performance he used to regularly climb onto the old man's knee for a scrap – infinitely preferable to his own breakfast. At one time, Joe Bellamy, his two sons and grandson all worked at Filwood Farm.

Alfred Pitman, labourer at Filwood, photographed in Whitchurch Lane, *c.* 1912. He walked daily from Bishopsworth whatever the weather.

Sarah Wyatt of Home Farm (see p. 14) married John Britton of Highridge Farm. This is a lovely character study from c. 1900 and tells us much about the style of dress preferred by Bishopsworth matrons at the turn of the century. The knobbly garden furniture, patterned oilcloth on the floor and the grandfather clock give a hint of the homely comfort and decorum within.

Highridge Farm, c. 1890, with two of the Britton girls. The old farmhouse was burnt down in the 1970s and all the out-buildings were converted into private residences.

John and Sarah Britton with their six daughters. From left to right, back row: Amy, Francis, Alice and Lil. Seated front: Nell, Mabel and Clare. A good-looking family – but a sad cloud hung over them. In later years Sarah was admitted for long periods to Dr Fox's private lunatic asylum in Brislington, and their only son, John – seen here behind his father – subsequently hanged himself in the barn.

Fanny Britton cut a splendid figure when she walked out with Mr Golledge, a Westbury vet, whom she eventually married.

Benjamin Wyatt of Home Farm married Alice Britton and became farmer of Brook Farm just outside the village where the Malago flowed under (and sometimes over) Whitchurch Lane. All their children died young, as is recorded on their headstones in St Peter's churchyard. This portrait dates from 1895 when leg-of-mutton sleeves made big women look even bigger.

Brook Farm, c. 1924, showing the low bridge over the Malago. Flooding regularly turned this field into a lake.

A winter scene at Brook Farm, *c.* 1930. Twenty years later the whole of the site was 'developed'.

By 1974, although the farmhouse survived as part of business premises, all the trees and the other farm buildings had disappeared. This is now the junction of Whitchurch Lane and Derham Road.

Susan Clapp, Bishopsworth's first post-girl, poses on a footbridge over Colliter's Brook in Hancock's Wood on Easter Sunday 1906. It is a pity we can't make out the title of her book.

We don't know his name of this man. He may have been MacPherson who was sent to deliver a telegram to Mr Sweet of Upton Farm. It was an extremely hot day and the lad had to push his bicycle all the way up to Dundry. At 8.30 p.m. the Central Post Office telephoned to say that MacPherson had not returned; where was he? He was eventually found fast asleep under a haystack. Mr Sweet had given him a mug of cider!

Mr Lloyd, postmaster and grocer, *c*. 1930. His shop was in Church Road near the junction with Whitchurch Lane. A post office extension was added on the right and managed separately by his daughter, a rather fierce matron lady called Miss Kate Lloyd. She was assisted by her niece, Elsie Clark. [M9].

In this 1935 postcard of the Church Road/Whitchurch Road junction, Lloyd's grocer's shop carries the name of his son-in-law, Bernard Clark, who for some reason was always called 'George'. Bernard Clark delivered to most houses in the lower village and collected the mail from the central sorting office, first on a bicycle, and later on a 'motorcycle combination with sidecar'. On the corner stands a public telephone box. You paid your penny to Elsie Clark over the counter and she would connect you to one of the dozen or so homes which had telephones. On the very conspicuous telegraph pole is a notice warning motorists to drive slowly through the village. The sign post reads 'DUNDRY $1\frac{1}{2}$; CHEW MAGNA $3\frac{1}{2}$; WHITCHURCH 2'.

Left: Edwin Wyatt joined the firm of Burgess and Ware in Marsh Street, Bristol, as clerk, later becoming cashier. This was in 1864, at the time of the American Civil War, and he was still working for the same firm until after the Second World War. Until considerably advanced in years, he would always walk to the office and back each day. Right: a portrait of Edwin, c. 1890, and Colston Knee who had been articled to the firm to learn conveyancing and accountancy. Colston was an unstable, indolent young man, and Edwin's diary, seen below, shows how hard he tried to keep Colston on the rails. He failed; Colston repeatedly failed his law exams, turned to drink, and eventually went to prison in 1915 for signing dud cheques.

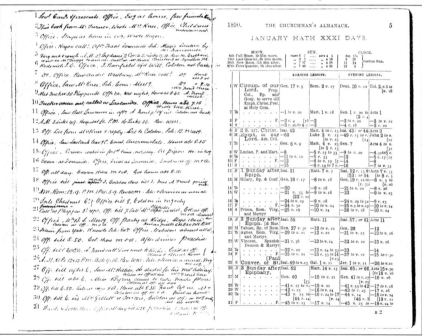

With meticulous precision, Edwin entered into the 'Churchman's Almanack' the weather, choir practices, meetings of the Parish Council and School Board, cricket matches and even the lesson in church – all in a single line of spidery writing – for every day for 27 years, beginning on 1 January 1890. It is an invaluable source of village history.

40

Bishopsworth cricket team, 1883. Edwin, holding the bat, was its secretary for many years. The names of the other members are not known but the photograph was evidently taken to celebrate the visit of the guest player, W.G. Grace (in striped blazer). They played in the field adjoining the churchyard – now part of Lakemead Gardens. [M27].

The cricket team about 1910. Edwin is second from the right, back row. Other members at the time were Bert Pursey, the village constable; Jack Reynolds and Fred Plumber, who worked for Wills; Fred Tutton, a butcher in West Street; Fred Cox and Charlie Gould who worked at Robinson's; and Tommy Cleak who was a clerk at Lysaght's, an engineering firm. The pavilion was burnt down in the early 1960s, though its foundations can be seen near the fence of Highridge Infant School.

142. Bishopsworth Church. *about 1905.*

St Peter's Church, *c.* 1905. The doorway then faced north. Since 1964 it has faced east after the vestry was built on this side. [SP].

The interior has not changed appreciably over the years. Under the direction of Walter Molesworth, a massive restoration was carried out between 1874 and 1884 which eventually proved more costly than the initial construction. The encaustic tiles are evident in this photo, *c.* 1930. They have long since been carpeted over.

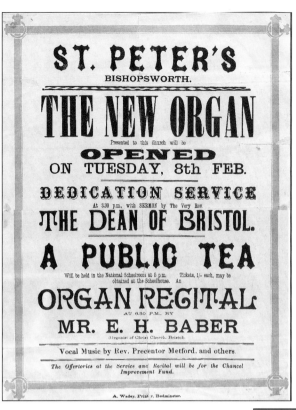

ST. PETER'S
BISHOPSWORTH.

THE NEW ORGAN
Presented to this Church will be

OPENED
ON TUESDAY, 8th FEB.

DEDICATION SERVICE
At 3.30 p.m., with SERMON by The Very Rev.

THE DEAN OF BRISTOL.

A PUBLIC TEA
Will be held in the National Schoolroom at 5 p.m.   Tickets, 1/- each, may be obtained at the Schoolhouse.   An

ORGAN RECITAL
AT 6.30 P.M., BY

MR. E. H. BABER
(Organist of Christ Church, Bristol.)

Vocal Music by Rev. Precentor Metford, and others.

The Offertories at the Service and Recital will be for the Chancel Improvement Fund.

A. Wadey, Print r, Bedminster.

The organ was given anonymously 'by a parishioner' in 1898. Only years later was it revealed that Edwin Wyatt was the donor.

Edwin never married and lived all his life with his brother, Arthur, farmer at Home Farm. This is a rather severe picture of Arthur. He could be ferocious with local boys who raided his orchard, but he was a genial, jovial soul, full of fun and a born entertainer, much in demand at village concerts. His devotion to church and choir was equal to that of Edwin. [MMW1]. Right: Arthur's wife, Lizzie, formerly of Prospect Cottage, Gifford's Hill.

The Wyatts and their relations adopted the four orphaned Millear daughters from Claverham: Edith, Agnes, Flora and Blanche. Edith Millear was housekeeper to Arthur and Edwin Wyatt.

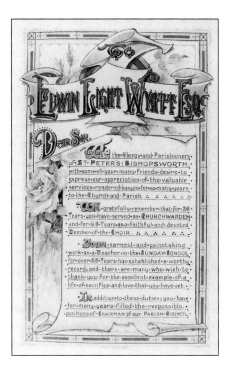

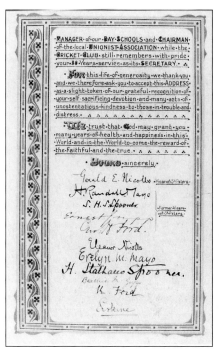

Four pages of the inscribed book presented to Edwin Wyatt in 1926 and signed by the entire village, in recognition of his 25 years as the churchwarden, 65 years with the church choir, devoted service as Chairman of the Parish Council and member of the School Board and 'many acts of enthusiastic kindness to those in trouble and distress'. The vignettes show Home Farm and St Peter's Church.

The Elm Tree Inn, which had recently been rebuilt by the Lodway Brewery Company, caught fire and burnt down on 6 March 1906. The Bedminster Fire Brigade was alerted but they were attending a much more serious outbreak in the city. It is said that certain regulars, who continued to drink steadily at the bar as it filled with smoke, coolly directed local people who rushed in with hosepipes to 'play it on the slate' in order to wipe clean the sums they owed the landlord, Nelson Harris! As a result of the fire, the Parish Council resolved to form their own fire brigade. A team was assembled by Mr Pobjoy, the captain, and a bright red fire tender, complete with brass bell, rescue ladders, hosepipes and paraffin lamps at each corner was acquired. It was kept at The Elm Tree and attended to several minor outbreaks before being taken over in the Second World War by the National Fire Service. [M6].

The Fire Brigade practising in Grange Road, c. 1907. The big Edwardian houses were then brand-new and 'The Elms' and 'Lynwood' were the last before the fields where Withywood estate now stands. The road was not officially adopted and metalled until the 1930s.

The village men and boys assemble to watch a fire practice at Primrose Villa, Grange Road, home of Mr Percy Newman, the Parish Clerk. In the background is the Men's Club at the junction of Church and Grange Roads (later Miss Bishop's shop). In 1909, the village was stunned by the news that Mr Newman had disappeared leaving a note that he was going to jump off Clifton Suspension Bridge. It later transpired that he had absconded to Australia with the parish rates!

George Froud of Castle Farm married Betsy Maynard, sister of Israel Maynard of Chestnut Court (see p. 29). Although technically from the parish of Long Ashton, the Frouds considered themselves Bishopsworth folk and played a major part in parish affairs.

Left: Alfred Froud, third son of George. His towering physique and personality dominated village affairs for half a century. He began his career as clerk in the Bedminster coal works, later becoming foreman when his father became contractor to the Turnpike Trust for repairs to the Bridgwater Road. He was a pillar of the church, one of the Guardians of the Poor Law Union, member of the Bedminster and Bristol School Boards, a member of Bishopsworth Parish Council and Councillor for Bedminster West, 1907-1913. Right: Captain Albert Froud, their eldest son, joined the merchant navy, served on board the SS *Argo* in the Crimean War and captained a number of ships in the Atlantic, Mediterranean and Black Sea routes before the loss of his ship *Parnassus*, c. 1878, put an end to his career. He died at Castle Farm, unmarried, in 1901 and has a magnificent headstone with chain and anchor in St Peter's churchyard.

Castle Farm about 1910. Apart from the ivy, it is relatively unchanged today and is the only one of the twenty-three former Bishopsworth farms still functioning.

This most eloquent of Bishopsworth photographs shows Alfred Froud and his wife, Elizabeth Hester, sister of Ben Hall of Filwood (p. 12), posing with the hay-makers at Castle Farm, *c.* 1910. They married late and had no children, but 'adopted' Flora Millear (centre, standing) who taught at the National School. At village concerts in the school, Alfred Froud was a great turn reciting 'Ben and the Butter' in broad 'Zummerset' dialect. Flora Millear cycled to school down a very narrow and deeply rutted King's Head Lane, often having to negotiate huge blackthorn branches thrown on the path by schoolboys to puncture her tyres. The child seated on the extreme right is Vic Hill. [M5, M33].

Dan Lovell with winch and pulley and seven labourers building a haystack at Colliter's Brook Farm, *c*. 1902. Many of the men were volunteers from Wills' cigarette factory or coal-miners who from ancient custom helped with the haymaking. [M6, M7, M8].

Roland Osmund, who succeeded Dan Lovell, haymaking at Colliter's Brook Farm, *c*. 1930. By then he had the benefit of power-driven elevators thus eroding the tradition of unpaid communal help which had survived for generations.

Cows were milked in the fields before 1914. Milking began at 4.00 a.m. By 5.30 a.m. the churns were full and loaded onto the milk cart. This had to be driven to the top of St Michael's Hill by 6.30 a.m. when the milk was still warm, for if it wasn't the smart people of Clifton would say it was yesterday's milk!

Colliter's Brook Farm from Yanleigh Lane in 1975. The building has escaped modernisation but the surroundings have been much altered by the Woodspring Country and Golf Club which was laid out in the early 1990s.

Mr Rossiter, a successful builder from the Mendips, built The Grange, a grand red-brick mansion, at the foot of Dundry Hill in 1899. He poses with his family in the porch in 1902 for this greetings card. He also built the Maternity Hospital on Clifton Downs. The stables are gone, but the house survives in a mutilated state as the Mendip Gate public house, boxed in on all sides by Withywood council estate. [M7].

George Wyatt, only son of Arthur and Lizzie Wyatt of Home Farm (p. 44) married Emily Rossiter of The Grange. This is their wedding photograph from 1897. George took up farming at Red House Farm but tragically Emily died in childbirth. Their daughter, Kathleen, survived.

Entrance to The Grange from Broadoak Hill, *c.* 1940.

View of The Grange (left) from Broadoak Hill, *c.* 1935. Further down Queen's Road, then only half its present width, is Oakhill Farm. The stables survive as a Scout HQ. Opposite are the first houses (all bungalows) in what, after 1970, was called Withywood. Bishopsworth, then still a very rural village, is in the middle distance, and beyond is Bedminster Down and the City.

Elizabeth Cooksley brought up eleven children in Pear Tree Cottage, one of many that once lined Queen's Road in the upper village. They took their water from the Malago which flowed behind the cottage. All eleven children climbed Dundry Hill to go to school. It was 2d a week for the eldest and 1d a week for all the others – 1d cheaper than at Bishopsworth. [M14].

Left: the Cooksleys reared pigs and until 1982 the pigsty still stood beside the road. Right: Elizabeth Cooksley's daughter, Lucy Young, lived in Pear Tree Cottage until her death in 1981 aged 91. Until then the cottage still had meat hooks in the ceiling, old fashioned wallpaper and a grandfather clock made by George Quarman of Temple Cloud. Modernisation has robbed the cottage of much of its character.

One of Elizabeth Cooksley's daughters, Ada, married Edwin Gallop and lived at Brook Cottage further down Queen's Road. He worked for the Great Western Railway (GWR).

Brook Cottage in 1975. Despite modernisation, it is the best preserved of all Bishopsworth's old cottages. Ada Gallop's daughters still live there and have witnessed many changes. Some 22 similar cottages have been demolished in Queen's Road alone and after the 1960s, Withywood council estate engulfed them on all sides.

This is Elizabeth Cooksley's husband, George Matthew, son of William Henry Cooksley who built the Rising Sun. Their son, William, who also became landlord, was known by some as 'Dayworks' because he had always refused to work on the night shift in the South Liberty Lane Colliery. Nicknames were common in Bishopsworth. 'Pinwire' Craddock, 'Mousey' Yates, 'Spragg' Garland, 'Whiteknob' Godfrey, 'Spadger' Wyatt (Edwin) and 'Jumper' Reeves (because he was one jump ahead of the police) are just a few. [M14].

The old Rising Sun, Queen's Road, was a cottage inn full of character. Crates of cider stood in the yard and on summer evenings the regulars relaxed on wooden benches. In the background is the roof of the stables of Oakhill Farm, now a Scout HQ. The old inn was demolished in the 1960s and replaced by a 'shoe-box' surrounded by acres of parking.

The Queen's Head about 1912. Although now rendered and modernised inside, it still preserves its original character. The photograph gives a good idea of Queen's Road before Gatehouse Avenue on the left and the rank of shops on the right replaced many of the ancient stone cottages. Notice the child playing in the road, the horse droppings and the inn sign which carried at that time the head of Queen Alexandra. [M12].

The King's Head from the rear, before 1928, when it was rebuilt for the first time, leaving a larger gap between the pub and Oldmead Farm through which King's Head Lane passed to the Bridgwater Road. The child is probably the daughter of Mr Reginald Weeks, the landlord from 1922. [M10, M34].

The original Congregational Church was built in 1828 and provided the only spiritual and educational needs of the village until the building of the National School and St Peter's Church in 1842. Understandably, there was much animosity between Church and Chapel, especially over the education of the children, which took a long time to die. In the background (to the right) are The Old Chapelle Cottages (see p. 18). [M7, SP].

Interior of the chapel. The congregation was served by the Bristol Congregational Itinerant Society who arranged for preachers to be sent out each Sunday. Among these were Thomas Sage, John Jones, J.G. Smart, Joseph Knapman and William Thomas. In 1915, Mr Joll was invited to take up the pastorate and under his ministry the church flourished.

The Congregational School was established in 1924 in an former Army hut erected in Grange Road, and in 1930 the Church (the present one) was rebuilt in Church Road, largely due to the dedication of Mr William J. Kew, Mr Ernest G. Iliffe and Mr Alexander Ayson. A doctors' surgery now occupies the site of the Congregational School Hall.

A Congregational Sunday School outing in 1904. On the extreme right is Alexander Ayson, who first came to Bristol from Exeter when he was 16. His employer, Mr Bird, invited him to Bishopsworth where the congregation had fallen to a mere handful. Mr Bird fell ill and died after delivering his first sermon as a lay-preacher but Alexander Ayson stayed on, and after 60 years of lay-preaching there were 90 children attending Sunday school and 78 members of the brotherhood and sisterhood. The lady seated second from the right is Mrs Ayson with her two baby daughters, Elsie May and Gladys, later Mrs Iliffe and Mrs Kew.

Bedminster Down in the nineteenth century was a rough district and considered an unsafe approach to Bishopsworth from Bristol. Village folk often took the longer route to the city via Headley Lane to avoid the unwelcome attention of the 'Bedminster Blinders' as the uncouth mining community was called. An enormous change was effected by the Primitive Methodists, pioneered by Joseph Jenkins, a converted miner, who called the first meetings in his tiny cottage about 1840. The cottage stood opposite the Zion Chapel which owes much to Joseph's zeal and was opened in 1863. He attended the first service and died four months later in 1864. To the left of his portrait is Mr S.C. Lovell, to the right Mrs Henry Hinton, Joseph's widow Elizabeth, and Mr Henry Hinton.

The first Zion Chapel, built from stone quarried on the site, contained twelve pews, enough to seat 150 people, but Joseph Jenkins' cottage opposite continued to be used for prayer meetings. The cottage was demolished c. 1900. [M2].

Funeral of Mr Fox, c. 1907, outside the second Zion Chapel built in 1890 alongside the first one which was later replaced by the Zion church hall and Sunday School room.

Sam Millsom's funeral on Bedminster Down Hill, 1912. He was a champion horse-dealer, selling his 'gryers' to the cavalries of pre-First World War Europe. Two Bedminster Down horses even pulled the Kaiser's carriage. The yard where the horses were exercised is now the site of the Downs' Supply. When he died, 40 carriages drawn by black horses lined up outside the paddock to accompany the coffin to Bishopsworth Church. He was buried in the churchyard. [M5].

William Woodhall (centre) came from Birmingham and married Mercy Evans (left, back row) of Barrow Gurney. They set up a butcher's shop at 66 Bedminster Parade and lived at Withywood Farm. They had six sons and three daughters. The eldest daughter Louisa (right, back row) married Alfred Daw Collard c. 1895 and, as Mrs Collard, ran their North Street butcher's shop for many years. Mr Collard's brother (left) is also in the photograph which dates from c. 1890.

Little William Woodhall at the age of 14 (extreme right in upper photo) was given his own butcher's shop on Bedminster Parade. It was little more than the width of a shop doorway. Four years later, in 1896, he died and there is a stone cross to his memory in St Peter's churchyard, just to the right of the gate from Fernsteed Road.

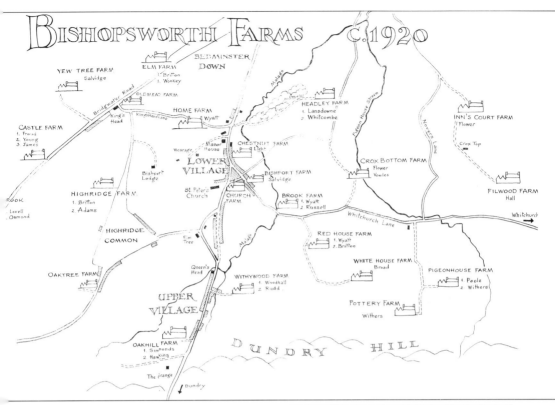

BISHOPSWORTH FARMS c.1920

YEW TREE FARM
Salvidge

ELM FARM
1. Britton
2. Wookey

BEDMINSTER DOWN

OLDMEAD FARM

HOME FARM
Wyatt

HEADLEY FARM
1. Lansdowne
2. Whitcombe

INN'S COURT FARM
Flower

Crox Top

CASTLE FARM
1. Freud
2. Young
3. James

King's Head

King's Head Lane

Vicarage

Manor House

CHESTNUT FARM
Light

LOWER VILLAGE

Bishport Lodge

St Peter's Church

BISHPORT FARM
Salvidge

CROX BOTTOM FARM
Flower
Vowles

FILWOOD FARM
Hall

HIGHRIDGE FARM
1. Britton
2. Adams

CHURCH FARM

BROOK FARM
1. Wyatt
2. Russell

RED HOUSE FARM
1. Wyatt
2. Britton

Whitchurch Lane

Whitchurch

ROOK
Lovell
Osmond

HIGHRIDGE COMMON

Elm Tree

WHITE HOUSE FARM
Broad

PIGEONHOUSE FARM
1. Poole
2. Withers

OAKTREE FARM

Queen's Head

WITHYWOOD FARM
1. Woodhall
2. Rudd

POTTERY FARM
Withers

UPPER VILLAGE

OAKHILL FARM
1. Simmonds
2. Hawkins

DUNDRY HILL

The Grange

Dundry

Withywood Farm, which gives Withywood its name, is seen in the centre of this photograph taken c. 1935. It was reached by a track from Queen's Road in the upper village which is now Gatehouse Avenue. The farm stood on a site now occupied by the Roman Catholic church and all its fields are built over. The farm may have taken its name from an old Dundry family by the name of Withy who owned land, including woods, on Dundry's northern slopes i.e. Mr Withy's Wood. [M25].

The Revd George Herbert Ford and his wife came to Bishopsworth in 1910. He extended the garden at the Vicarage to make a tennis court and 'tennis parties at the Vicarage' in his day became the rage. [M11, MMW1].

Bishopsworth Parish Magazine.

VOL. I.　　　JANUARY, 1911.　　　No. 1.

SAINTS' DAYS AND HOLY DAYS.

January 1st, Feast of the Circumcision ; January 6th, Feast of the Epiphany ; January 25th, Feast of the Conversion of S. Paul.

VICAR'S LETTER.

My dear Friends,

As I take up my pen to write to you in the first issue of our Parish Magazine, there comes to my mind the old Latin watchwords—" Respice ! Inspice ! Aspice !—Look back ! look within ! look forward !

Look back ! Well, as I look back on the past year, I am full of thankfulness ; thankfulness to God for the manifold tokens of His loving kindness, and for the kind way in which Mrs. Ford and myself have been received during the first year of our work in this parish. We have experienced nothing but kindness on all hands, and we seem to have already established that mutual good feeling which is so essential, it we are to work together for the building up of the Church of Christ in this parish.

Look within ! As we look within, I am sure that all of us must be conscious of many failures and shortcomings. Unless we are dissatisfied with our present attainments, our ideal—the standard at which we are aiming—must be a very low one. Our attitude must ever be that of the great Apostle—" Not as though I had already attained, or were already perfect, but this one thing I do, forgetting the things which are behind, and reaching forth unto those things which are before, I press towards the mark ! We need not be morbidly cast down because of our failures, for—

He who climbs must count to fall ;
But each new fall shall find him climbing still.

It is not what we *are*, but what we are *striving to be*, that God looks at. God does not despair of what is imperfect, because it is imperfect. He views all of us who are putting our trust in Christ and fighting against sin, not as we are, but as we are becoming ; not by the level of our present attainment, but by the character and direction of our movement. As we look within then at our spiritual state and condition can we see progress

Bishopsworth Parish Magazine.

VOL. V.　　　MARCH, 1915.　　　No. 3.

MOTTO FOR 1915—" WATCH AND PRAY."

My dear Friends,

The awful war still drags on its weary length, and the vast toll of life is being increased day by day. We must not slacken our prayers for those in the midst of such terrible carnage and for those in such imminent danger on the seas. During Lent the Intercessions will be taken before the Address at the Friday evening Service at 7-45. I notice a tendency, especially among our younger Communicants, to neglect the other Sunday Services. This must not be. Unless we are sufficiently in earnest to make the utmost use of the Sunday as a day of prayer and worship it is a grave question whether we are mete partakers of the Holy Mysteries.

The collections throughout the day on Sunday, March 14th, will be given to the Diocesan Mission. Canon Everingham will preach to Men in the afternoon at 3-15.

I am glad to notice such good attendances at our Lent Services. I trust they will be maintained.

I remain,

Your faithful Friend and Pastor,

GEORGE H. FORD.

BELGIAN REFUGEES.

The household now consists of a mother, a married son and his wife and one little child, a daughter and baby, the little child of another son still at Ostend, and a lad of sixteen or seventeen. The married son and the lad have both got work in Bristol. The man earns 18/- a week and the lad 8/-. The Committee feel that the time has come for them to cater for themselves. At the meeting held on February 22nd it was decided to allow the married couple 2/- a week, thus making their weekly income £1; and to allow the others £1, making their weekly income up to 28/-. The Committee will continue to pay the rent of the house. Our weekly expenses will now amount to £1 6s. 6d. We hope that contributors will continue their kind contributions, though at a reduced rate. It is reckoned that half the amount hitherto given weekly will now be sufficient to meet our liabilities. The Committee have placed £20 on deposit at the Bank, to be given to the two families when they are able to return to Belgium. The little boy who was born on January 29th was very delicate from birth and only lived three weeks. He was buried on February 23rd in our Churchyard.

Left: in January 1911 the Revd Ford began the Parish magazine and it has flourished ever since. This is the first page of the first number. Right: a page from the March 1915 magazine after Revd Ford had summoned a meeting to consider what efforts the village could make to accommodate the stream of refugees fleeing from alleged German 'atrocities' in Belgium. In due course, two vacant cottages in Chapel Lane were made available to the Sys family from Ostende.

64

The Revd Jupp succeeded Mr Ford in 1917. In this church choir from 1920 were from left to right, back row: -?-, Morris Simmons, -?-, Frank Elverd, -?-, -?-. Middle row: Edward Pobjoy, Mr Moon (Headmaster), Arthur Wyatt, Mr Jupp, Edwin Wyatt, Cecil Hill and his brother, Gerald Hill. Front row: Reg Carter, -?-, -?-, Sidney Harver, Ken Bowden.

Mrs Jupp began the ladies choir c. 1920. From left to right, back row: Maud Fear, Elsie Simmons, -?-, Flo Plummer, Mr Jupp, Lily Sidders, Rene Pobjoy, Lily Birmingham. Second row: Lily Peak, Daisy Vowles, Winnie Birmingham, Mrs Jupp, Mary Groves, -?-, Flo Powell. In front: Doris Simmons, Phyllis Tutton.

Bishopsworth National School group with Mr Moon, *c.* 1905. Charlie Gallop is in the front row, but we don't have the names of the others. One of the little girls related later (*c.* 1978): 'Mr Moon was a strict disciplinarian. At times he used to have a brainstorm, go quite scatty and strike his desk with the cane.' [M3, M4].

Mrs Moon, —
Head-mistress of Infants School,
+ Church Organist for many years

Mrs Moon was headmistress of the Infants and also church organist. Morris ('Mark') Simmons wrote: 'I started in Mrs Moon's class. I got on well at first. We always used to have plenty of fun and knew it was time to go home when that well-known hymn was sung, *Now the day is over night is drawing nigh.* Once, while escaping from angry mothers whose children he had caned because no one owned up to who had fired a pea-shooter at him during his after-lunch nap, he knocked Mrs Moon over and went and hid in the church. The children used to chant behind him:

'Mr Moon is a nice young man
He tries to teach us all he can,
Reading, writing and arithmetic,
He doesn't forget to give us the stick.
When he does he makes us dance
Out of England into France
Out of France and into Spain
Over the hills and back again.'

Bishopsworth School, c. 1920. From left to right, back row: George Torrington, Stanley Newman, Nelson Bishop, Norman Gould, Ted Morton, George Beale, Tom Davey, Henry Kew, Albert Cox. Third row: Ivy Maidstone, Clarice Gadd, Nellie Moreton, Iris Marsh, Cora Tuckfield, Cicely Elverd, Nina Bishop, Nora Higgins, Ella Lewis, Marion Vowles. Second row: Ivy Simmons, Louisa Clark, Kathleen Chivers, Gladys Groves, Lottie Moreton, Ida Harvey, Ethel Reeves, Florrie Valentine, Phyllis Gallop. Front row: Charles French, Walter Beaton, William Elms, George Marshall, Leslie Oldfield, Leonard Garland, Leonard Oldfield, Clifford Coles.

Bishopsworth School, c. 1930, in the time of headmaster 'Sammy' Lewis. From left to right, back row: Terry Davies, Tony Hamblin, Albert Leach, Arthur Patch, Sidney Blackmoon. Third row: Ivy Lock, Jane Withers, Iris Hill, Audrey Oldfield, Edna Harris, Joan Cox, Dolly Pitman. Second row: Edna Reeves, Vera Eley, Joyce Hallas, Mr Lewis, Beryl Milkins, Doris Hunt, Joan Small, Graham Morland. Front row: Alfred Beale, Fred Cole, Stanley Weeks, Joan Howell, Jim Rocket, George Kew, Arthur Crombie.

Joe Simmons, Bishopsworth postman, heard that one of his best mates, Charlie Lukins, had been killed in France in the First World War. He took off his postman's clothes and sat on his bed with tears in his eyes. 'I'm not going to stay home,' he said. His parents pleaded with him not to go but he joined the 6th Gloucesters and went to the Western Front. He was seriously wounded in the thigh, was invalided home, patched up and passed fit to go abroad again. 'On no account tell my mother or my sisters,' he said. 'I'll be back next week,' he told them, 'I'm only having a check up'. He was reported missing, presumed killed, on 5 October 1917 at Ypres. Mrs Simmons never gave up hope that one day he would come walking up that cinder path to Gaston Cottage. [M31, M32, M33].

Sidney Hamblin was called up from 'Bishopslea' in Church Road into the Duke of Cornwall's Light Infantry in the autumn of 1917. After basic training he was posted to Flanders. 'We don't fire at Fritz, 'tis useless as we can't see him,' he wrote. 'I am afraid 'tis only too true about the mud, up to our waist in places...'. Rushed to the Amiens sector to halt a new German offensive in March 1918, his unit was overwhelmed and he was last sighted lying beside a ditch near the village of Addicourt firing from the shelter of a small tree. A shell burst on the survivors and none of them was ever seen alive again.

Albert Hill was a coal-haulier at the South Liberty Pit and lived in a cottage near the King's Head. The Hill family group, c. 1906, shows, from left to right, back row: Charlie, Maud, Father, Mabel, Albert and Joe. Front row: George, Sam, Mother (Tillie), Victor, Eddie, Bill. Most of the sons worked in the pit, or hauled coal, sometimes waiting all night for the coal to come up, for the first-comers could be certain of work. Victor, the youngest, was sent home by his father at 8.00 a.m. to have his breakfast and went straight off to school, his hands still black with coal dust. Vic Hill died in 1996.

The Hill family, 1915. From left to right, back row: the three Latham brothers billeted on the Hills while assembling mules from the Mendips for shipment to France; Charlie Hill (17), who, a few months later, lied about his age and joined the Royal Navy. Only ten weeks after joining HMS *Indefatigable*, as a stoker, he lost his life at the Battle of Jutland; Joe Hill, who served in the Royal Garrison Artillery; Henry Reynolds (Maud's husband). Middle row: Mabel, Billy, Father and Mother, George and Maud. Front row: Eddie, Vic (with Teddy) and Sam. Brother Albert was away on the Western Front serving in the Light Infantry.

Sidney Hall (see p. 32) seen here seated with his parents and sisters, Win and Dorothy, and his brother Anthony at Filwood Farm. He had passed through Bristol Grammar School and University with honours and was working as an engineer for Stothert and Pitt when the First World War broke out. He enlisted with the Royal Naval Division, was promoted to Sergeant and posted to Deal to train his men.

Left: in March 1915 Dorothy and Anthony Hall saw Sidney off on HMS *Somali* at Avonmouth docks. Between train and ship, that last, brief hour was spent sticking stamps on the letters his unit had written home. He took his leave, did not look back or re-appear at the rail. 'Those who look back are not fit for the Kingdom of Heaven,' thought Dorothy at the time. Right: Sidney (extreme right) leading his men ashore at Lemnos in the Aegean. It was now clear that his ship was bound for Gallipoli.

After three months relentless toil against unassailable Turkish positions, Sidney, now Sergeant Major, was returning to base on 27 July to collect supplies for his men, when a shell from a battery on the Asian shore of the Darndanelles killed him and his horse. His pocket book and letters narrating those last desperate weeks were returned to his family and have since been used in a book about him (unpublished). His grave (arrowed) was marked by a stone cross cut out of the cliffs under fire by his men at Cape Hellas. He was one of the 27 young men of Bishopsworth to die in the First World War, with 31 perishing in the Second. [M34].

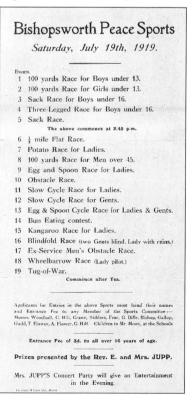

Bishopsworth Peace Sports

Saturday, July 19th, 1919.

Events.

1. 100 yards Race for Boys under 13.
2. 100 yards Race for Girls under 13.
3. Sack Race for Boys under 16.
4. Three-Legged Race for Boys under 16.
5. Sack Race.

The above commence at 2.45 p.m.

6. ¼ mile Flat Race.
7. Potato Race for Ladies.
8. 100 yards Race for Men over 45.
9. Egg and Spoon Race for Ladies.
10. Obstacle Race.
11. Slow Cycle Race for Ladies.
12. Slow Cycle Race for Gents.
13. Egg & Spoon Cycle Race for Ladies & Gents.
14. Bun Eating contest.
15. Kangaroo Race for Ladies.
16. Blindfold Race (two Gents blind, Lady with reins.)
17. Ex-Service Men's Obstacle Race.
18. Wheelbarrow Race (Lady pilot.)
19. Tug-of-War.

Commence after Tea.

Applicants for Entries in the above Sports must hand their names and Entrance Fee to any Member of the Sports Committee:— Messrs. Woodhall, C. Hill, Crane, Sidders, Fear, G. Iliffe, Bishop, Gallop, Gadd, T. Flower, A. Flower, G. Hill. Children to Mr. Moon, at the Schools

Entrance Fee of 3d. to all over 16 years of age.

Prizes presented by the Rev. E. and Mrs. JUPP.

Mrs. JUPP'S Concert Party will give an Entertainment in the Evening.

Alice Gill, sextoness of St Peter's Church for nearly half a century. As a small girl, living in a labourer's cottage in Whitchurch Lane, she dreamed of one day becoming village sextoness. She went into service at the age of 14, and when her employer died in 1900 she returned to Bishopsworth to find the post she had dreamed of vacant. For a weekly wage of 1/6d, she cleaned the church, tolled the bell and registered births, marriages and deaths. She became an expert on village affairs and people consulted her as they would an oracle.

Left: Alice Gill outside her cottage in Whitchurch Lane. She was a large lady – seventeen stone – and children stood much in awe of her. 'She always had a clout for us,' said one of them, but there was another side to her. 'She was a great big happy woman, always ready to lend a hand, be sympathetic to troubles and give wholesome advice.' Most summer evenings she could be seen sitting on a low wall shelling peas into a pail for Dolly Powell who had many children. She died in 1947 and is buried in the churchyard although there is no monument to her. However, as St Paul's Cathedral is for Christopher Wren, St Peter's is Alice Gill's memorial; 'If you seek my monument, then look around'. [M3, SP].

Mrs Pitman succeeded Alice Gill as sextoness, and rang the church bell when the war ended in 1945. She and her daughter, Winnie Elverd, who followed her, lived at this cottage in Chapel Lane. Here she made bookings and collected money for weddings, found the correct graves for burials, cleaned the brass, arranged the flowers and washed the church linen.

Mrs ELVERD. *Parish Clerk & Sextoness*

ARRANGEMENTS FOR BAPTISM & WEDDINGS

BANNS AND WEDDINGS
THE OFFICE
The Church Hall, Headley Rd
MONDAY & WEDNESDAY   7pm - 8.30pm

BAPTISM & CHURCHING
18, CHAPEL ROAD
ON
TUESDAY 10AM - 5 PM   WEDNESDAY 10AM - 2 PM

AND IN THE CHURCH ON
FRIDAY 10AM - 5PM

When the office of sextoness was discontinued, c. 1973, the board remained outside her cottage until it was demolished about four years later. It was rescued by the Malago Society and preserved as part of the village's history.

73

The Gardiners. Mrs Caroline Gardiner and her three daughters, Emma, Fanny and Jessie, came from Bishport Lodge to live at Chestnut Court. They taught in the Sunday school and made red flannel petticoats to give to poor villagers at Christmas. Only Jessie married, but she died young and her daughter Jessie Sawtell (standing) was brought up by her aunts, Emma (sitting) and Fanny (see below).

When the Misses Gardiner entertained village ladies to tea, Jessie sat on a tuffet working at her embroidery and was never expected to speak until spoken to. From time to time her aunts would turn to her and say, 'Isn't that so, Jessie?'. Jessie would reply demurely, 'Yes, Aunt Emma' or 'Yes, Aunt Fanny'.

Left: in 1928, Jessie Sawtell, well into middle age and now living alone, was proposed to by Mr James Clark, aged 79, a lay-preacher from Redfield, who with others had been invited to tea at Chestnut Farm by Mrs Light. Jessie, 'The Good Lady' as she was known for her charitable work, was helping out as usual. 'When I received your letter,' wrote Miss Sawtell, 'I did what Hezikiah did of old; I laid it before the Lord'. Instead of a wedding reception and honeymoon they gave a treat to the Sunday School children of Moorfields. [M11]. Right: James Clark was rather a handful, given to loud grunts and snorts in church, falling out of his pew, or roaming around the village in his pyjamas. When his toe was amputated he insisted that it be buried in hallowed ground and it was accordingly laid to rest in St Peter's churchyard. The rest of him, and Jessie, in due course, followed.

William Gardiner, landowner, was Jessie's uncle. His pursuit of Miss Dorothy Hall of Filwood Farm, with carriage waiting at the gate, horses stamping and snorting, was only marginally less dramatic than episodes from Wuthering Heights and was related with relish by that lady to the end of her days. Miss Hall never did marry; he did, unhappily.

Melbourne Lodge, an attractive regency house, stood on the rising ground now occupied by Bishopsworth Police Station. It was the setting of the wedding, c. 1924, of Cherry Bryant, who had been brought up by Mr G.E. Iliffe in Grange Road following the death of her mother, and Mr Harry Baxter from Swindon. Regrettably, we cannot identify any of the guests – perhaps they were all 'his people' from Swindon. Melbourne Lodge was then the home of Dr Roberts.

A photograph dating from between 1936 and 1939, when the house was the home of the last occupants, the Plumpton family. An elegant verandah surrounded the house at ground floor level. During the Second World War it was left unoccupied, damaged by incendiary bombs and demolished soon afterwards.

Ostende Cottage (left) which was built c. 1926 by Edwin Wyatt for his sister Clara Hall (see p. 15), then widowed, and her daughter Dorothy. Her son, Anthony, married about this time and took over the management of Filwood Farm. The house was named after a visit by Edwin and Dorothy to the port of that name and the First World War battlefields. West End cottage (right) was the home of Mrs Rossiter and her daughter for many years. To the right, through the trees, Melbourne Lodge is just visible. Ostende and West End cottages were the first houses built in Bishopsworth after the First World War.

From Headley Park, still undeveloped, the scene in 1926 was incredibly rural. The cottages still exist but are today locked in high-density suburbia. Immediately opposite stands Bishopsworth Library, the Police Station to the left. The gated track in the valley still runs through the top end of Manor Woods and originally connected Bishopsworth Road with Headley Farm.

PC Hill and his family in the garden of 'West View', Bishopsworth's first police station, c. 1912. Behind Mrs Hill are the old barns belonging to Church Farm. They still exist opposite St Peter's Church. The little girls are Ida and Alice ('Queenie'), who as Mrs Queenie Gallop appears in the photo on p. 90. The boys are Gerald and Cecil who appear in the choir photograph c. 1920 (see p. 65) and Hill and Lidbury's Waggon works (p. 80). It was a tradition that Bishopsworth policemen liked their drink. PC Hill's predecessor, PC Joe Pursey, used to get his friends to hide a pint of beer for him behind the church wall. PC Hill was not so lucky. He was found out and obliged to leave the force.

'West View', the first police station, later the home of Mr Joe Sidders, who ran an upholstery business in the greenhouse and had a sideline as a taxi man. His first taxi was a 'Scout', bought in 1929 for £12. Bright green outside with red leather seats inside and a very square upright chassis, it had large, old-fashioned, brass carbide lamps and batteries on the running boards between the mudguards. It was Bishopsworth's first motor-car. 'We thought we were lord and lady with that,' said Mrs Sidders. He charged 3d a mile and special terms for weddings. Later he exchanged the 'Scout' for an 'Overland', then he had a Hillman, then a Wolseley, in fact six Wolseleys, one after another, till he retired in 1962. 'West View' was demolished c. 1968.

78

PC Parsons (left) meets his opposite number from Whitchurch at Filwood Farm, c. 1929, to exchange information about poachers, vagrants, gypsies and drunks. On other appointed days he would walk to the parish boundaries to collect similar information from the Chew Magna and Long Ashton police constables. The little girls, Hilda and Jackie Page, spent their summer holidays at Filwood Farm with their adopted 'Auntie', Dorothy Hall. In due course, 'Auntie Dor' became everyone's good aunt.

Africa Villa, Grange Road (on the left) became Bishopsworth's second police station in 1922. The photograph dates from 1975, not long after it had lost the upper part of its bay windows with projecting conical roof and finial. This has been the fate of most of the splendid Edwardian houses in Grange Road. [M4, M27].

Cecil Hill and Arthur Lidbury had fought in the First World War. In the economic depression that followed, Edwin Wyatt helped them set up a waggon works in the out-buildings of Church Farm. They specialised in making draymen's carts and on the occasion of this photograph they constructed an enormous brace of wheels for export to North America for transporting timber. St Peter's Church, where the wheels were blessed, is just visible to the right of the picture.

Hill and Lidbury's waggon works continued to make horse-drawn vehicles until after the Second World War. It was succeeded by the North Somerset Vehicle Works, and today the buildings – almost the oldest in the village – are appreciably the same as when this photograph was taken in 1975. Davis Roofing Ltd currently (1996) use the premises.

Church Road junction with Whitchurch Lane, *c.* 1934. To the right, Bernard Clark's general store and post office; centre, Montana Villa, the home briefly of Joe Brock, the controversial chairman of Bishopsworth Parish Council. His sharp practices, cutting language and radical politics made him so unpopular that he was hanged in effigy opposite the Elm Tree in 1899. So many rocks were thrown at the figure that they blocked the road. On the left are some of the eight lavish Edwardian semi-detached villas built by Walter Chivers – it was said one for each of his eight daughters when they married. In the event five of the eight married, none lived there, though his nephew, Mr Bert Chivers, occupied one, and his widow is still (1996) living there. All the houses on the right were demolished for road-widening in the 1960s and 70s.

Bernard Clark used to deliver groceries to the lower village in a cart pulled by a little horse called Dolly. The stable was in the wall between the general store and Montana Villa, immediately opposite the home of Mr Bert Chivers' wife, Ruth, who painted this *c.* 1937. One day, Dolly was found collapsed in her stable and after that Bernard Clark delivered in a van.

The Revd Nicolls and his wife. He came to Bishopsworth from St John's, Bedminster, in 1927. To their great sorrow their only daughter, Bridget Mary, had left home to go on the stage. In London she met and fell in love with a nobleman. He was already married and divorce was out of the question. She had two children by him and was expecting a third when on Christmas Eve, 1928, she fell critically ill. Mr Nicolls was preparing for Christmas services, so Mrs Nicolls went to her daughter's bedside. It was too late. She died and so did the child.

Bridget was buried on the right of the church path just inside the gate. For months afterwards a taxi came from Temple Meads every Saturday, bringing a gentleman in deep mourning. He covered the grave with flowers and fell upon it in a state of inconsolable grief.

With great secrecy, for the name of the gentleman has never been divulged, a great painting from his collection was presented to the Church, 'In loving memory of B.M.N.' It is the Virgin and Child with Saint Elizabeth and reputed to be by Nicholas Poussin. The painting was sold in 1993 to help pay for underpinning the church's foundations and it has been replaced by a replica, though the gorgeous gilded frame could not be reproduced for the modern copy. Mr and Mrs Nicolls gave the Children's Corner in memory of their daughter and left the parish in 1930. [SP].

Left: Annie Davey wrote on the back of this postcard, 'To my friend Lon with Best Wishes' (c. 1915). 'In the event of my death,' wrote Sergeant Lon Upham on the same card, 'this photo will be forwarded to Miss A. Davey, Queen's Road, Bishopsworth'. The card was returned to Annie. Ten years later she married Alf Howe whose family lived on Broadoak Hill. She was 38. He was 26. He was her first cousin and there were no children. Here are Annie Howe and Alf (with cigarette) in the door of the Stoke Inn, Chew Stoke, where Alf was licensee, 1929-30.

The cottage in Queen's Road where Annie and Alf lived c. 1975, before it was modernised.

In 1924, Annie bought a memo book in which to keep accounts. Alf was a likeable chap but never kept a job for long and was frequently fined for speeding. In 1936 she started writing a diary in the memo book and kept it going for the next 34 years until a few weeks before her death in 1970. Two pages are reproduced here.

Annie and her father on Dundry Hill, c. 1939. Annie never travelled much further than the garden gate but recorded events, great and small, in glorious juxtaposition. Her dental problems, pets' ailments and Alf's traffic offences are accorded as much importance as World Wars, the downfall of governments and dictators, the Battle of Britain and the bombing of British cities. It is also a major source of Bishopsworth history – much of it too salacious for publication. [M20, M21, M22, M23, M24].

Gifford's Hill, 1935. The approach to St Peter's Rise and Headley Park is under construction. Many telegraph poles trailing new copper wires are very much in evidence. Prospect Cottage is on the right. The patch of ground in front is now occupied by Bishopsworth Library.

Prospect Cottage, c. 1920. It was the birthplace of Walter Beaton whose milk-round from Lower Grove Farm, Dundry, was patronised by most Bishopsworth people.

Grange Road/Church Road junction, *c.* 1920. The Men's Club on the corner, built *c.* 1914, had become a grocer's shop and has had many uses since. Roads were still unmetalled and sufficiently empty for children to play with their hoops or cruise on roller-skates non-stop from Highridge Common to the foot of Gifford's Hill. The houses on the left lost their railings to armaments in the Second World War.

Children in Church Road, *c.* 1935. The new Congregational Church (1930) is just out of the picture to the left; and on the right a single-storied extension to the Men's Club, now gone, served as part of the shop.

The first Greyhound bus service from Bristol to the Elm Tree Inn, Bishopsworth, began in 1922. Solid rubber-tyred wheels had to negotiate ruts, pot-holes and narrow lanes lined with sprawling hawthorn hedges.

The Greyhound company were compelled to withdraw their service when the Ball brothers, Frank and Stivvie, launched the Dundry Pioneer in 1923. The Balls slashed fares from 5d to 1d and the Greyhound retreated. This was the Balls' second bus, a 24-seater Dennis. It was painted brown with the words 'DUNDRY PIONEER' picked out in cream.

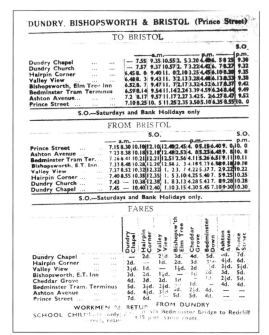

DUNDRY, BISHOPSWORTH & BRISTOL (Prince Street)

TO BRISTOL

	a.m.			p.m.			S.O. p.m.
Dundry Chapel	— 7.55 9.35 10.55	2. 5 3.20 4.20 6. 5 8 25	9.30
Dundry Church	— 7.57 9.37 10.57	2. 7 3.22 4.22 6. 7 8.27	9.32
Hairpin Corner	6.45 8. 0 9.40 11. 0	2.10 3.25 4.25 6.10 8.30	9.35
Valley View	6.48 8. 3 9.43 11. 3	2.13 3.28 4.28 6.13 8.33	9.38
Bishopsworth, Elm Tree Inn	6.52 8. 7 9.47 11. 7	2.17 3.32 4.32 6.17 8.37	9.42
Bedminster Tram Terminus	6.59 8.14 9.54 11.14	2.24 3.39 4.59 6.24 8.44	9.49
Ashton Avenue	7.2 8.17 9.57 11.17	2.27 3.42 5. 2 6.27 8.47	9.52
Prince Street	7.10 8.25 10. 5 11.25	2.35 3.50 5.10 6.35 8.55	10. 0

S.O.—Saturdays and Bank Holidays only.

FROM BRISTOL

	S.O. a.m.			p.m.			S.O. p.m.
Prince Street	7.15 8.30 10.10 12.10	12.40 2.45 4. 05 5.15 6.40 9. 0	10. 0
Ashton Avenue	7 23 8.38 10.18 12.18	12.48 2.53 4. 8 5.23 6.48 9. 8	10. 8
Bedminster Tram Ter.	7 26 8 41 10.21 12.21	12.51 2.56 4.11 5.26 6.51 9.11	10.11
Bishopsworth, E.T. Inn	7.33 8.48 10.28 12.28	12.58 3. 3 4.18 5.33 6.58 9.18	10.18
Valley View	7.37 8.52 10.32 12.32	1. 23. 7 4.22 5.37 7. 2 9.22	10.22
Hairpin Corner	7.40 8.55 10.35 12.35	1. 53.10 4.25 5.40 7. 5 9.25	10.25
Dundry Church	7.43 — 10.38 12.38	1. 8 3.13 4.28 5.43 7. 8 9.28	10.28
Dundry Church	7.45 — 10.40 12.40	1.10 3.15 4.30 5.45 7.10 9-30	10.30

S.O.—Saturdays and Bank Holidays only.

FARES

	Dundry Chapel	Hairpin Corner	Valley View	Bishopsw'th Elm Tree	Cheddar Grove	Bedminster Down	Ashton Avenue	Prince Street
Dundry Chapel		2d.	2½d.	3d.	4d.	5d.	6d.	7d.
Hairpin Corner	2d.	—	1d.	2d.	3d.	3½d.	4½d.	6d.
Valley View	2½d.	1d.	—	1¼d.	2d.	2½d.	3½d.	5½d.
Bishopsworth, E.T. Inn	3d.	2d.	1¼d.	—	1d.	1d.	3d.	5d.
Cheddar Grove	4d.	3d.	2d.	1d.		1d.	2½d.	5d.
Bedminster Tram. Terminus	5d.	3½d.	2½d.	1d.	1d.	—	4d.	4d.
Ashton Avenue	6d.	4½d.	3½d.	3d.	2½d.	4d.	—	—
Prince Street	7d.	6d.	5d.	5d.	5d.	4d.		

WORKMEN 9d. RETURN FROM DUNDRY
SCHOOL CHILDREN only ... via Bedminster Bridge to Redcliff
... 4 15 p.m. same route

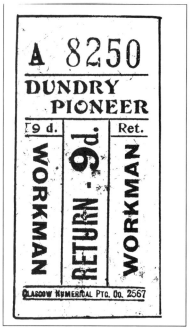

A 8250

DUNDRY PIONEER

9d.   RETURN - 9d.   Ret.

WORKMAN   WORKMAN

GLASGOW NUMERICAL PTG. CO. 2567

In the 1930s Stivvie (right) and Frank (left) added two more buses to their fleet, both Bedfords. Their sister Aggie was pressed into service as a 'clippie' and during the rush hour, when both Bedfords ran together, she would collect the fares on one, hop off and attend to the other. Preference was given to Dundry and Bishopsworth people and it became a reliable and much loved institution. It kept such regular time that people set their watches by it and Stivvie could always be counted on to do the occasional shopping errand or collect doctors' prescriptions for regulars. In winter weather, the whole community would rally to dig the 'Pioneer' out of snowdrifts or push it round Storm Point corner. The service came to an end in 1950 when the Ball brothers retired and the route was taken over by the Bristol Tramway Company. [M3].

Miss Bullen, a member of the Wills family, tries her luck on the skittle alley after opening the fête in the garden of the old Vicarage, Bishopsworth, c. 1950. To the extreme left is the Revd Marshall Hall, then Mrs 'Queenie' Gallop and Sam Hall from Bedminster Down. We have not been able to identify the gent with the pipe, however.

W.J. Kew and family lived at The Grange after the Rossiters (see p. 52). He was the builder of most of Uplands and Bedminster Down in the 1930s. Donald Road, Garth Road, Ellis Road, Alexandra Road and Tugela Road were named after members of his family and business associates. W.J. Kew and his wife were pillars of the Congregational Church and very public spirited members of the community. He opened his house to refugees from the bombing raids on Bedminster, 1940-42, and frequently in the late 1940s held garden parties for local people.

A garden party at The Grange, c. 1951. Not long afterwards Mr and Mrs Kew retired to Brockley. He was a confirmed teetotaller and refused an offer for his property from the brewery. He accepted an offer from another buyer, who in turn sold it on to the brewery and, to his mortification, the new owners obtained a licence to turn it into a public house. Despoiled of its beautiful garden and many of its ornate features, including the pretty conservatory above the porch, it is now The Mendip Gate. [M7].

Miss Clara Cox in her bath chair. She kept a little sweet shop in Whitchurch Lane between Swiss Cottage and Alice Gill's cottage. Behind the hedge are the labourers' cottages belonging to Red House Farm, which are the only cottages in the lower village to survive relatively unchanged.

Chapel Lane takes its name from the medieval chapel of ease built here in 1190. On the left is the cottage of Winnie Elverd, village sextoness. On the right, just out of the picture, is Swiss Cottage built by Edwin Wyatt in memory of his annual walking holidays in Switzerland before the First World War. It was the home of his friends the Hill family, Gerald and his sister Queenie who married Charlie Gallop. At the end of the lane is the village smithy (see p. 18). Geralds's brother Cecil lived here with his family until c. 1960 when most of the site was cleared for Bishopsworth Swimming Pool.

Mr Bagnell and his sister, Mrs Crawford of Bishport Lodge, a large ivy-covered house which stood in the fields on a site now occupied by Elm Hayes Old People's Home. He had been the mixer for George's Brewery, which may explain his splendid invalid carriage.

Canon Edward Marshall Hall became Vicar of Bishopsworth in 1936. He was an immensely good-looking man and incredibly active. He had a particular gift for appealing to the young and he was for ever playing cricket with the village lads, leaping five-bar gates, romping across the Common with the children, organising fancy dress carnivals and boys camps to the Isle of Wight. He was called up for war service in 1940, was Padre at the battle of Monte Casino and returned to the village in 1945. He set up the first temporary church in Hartcliffe and founded the first scout troop at Pottery Farm. There was much competition among the ladies for his affections and it was a great shock to most of them when he married Evelyn Crawford of Bishport Lodge, for she was many years his senior. This is a wedding day photograph and, true to character, the marriage certificate sticks crazily out of his pocket! They left the village in 1954. [M10, SP].

The Revd Langley-Webb clutches the hand of Mrs Burden (of the Burden Neurological Institute) who came to open the new Church Hall in 1936. For months, sales of work and other fund-raising projects had piled up the pennies to pay for this and it was a great day for Bishopsworth when the building on the corner of Whitchurch Lane and Headley Road was completed. It served many useful functions in its time; it was the HQ of the Bishopsworth Home Guard in the Second World War. Completely rebuilt, it is today the Kingdom Hall of the Jehovah's Witnesses. In the audience, from left to right, front row: Mr Roy Elton, Mrs Langley-Webb and, extreme right in pigtails, her daughter. Behind her, in a round hat, is Mrs Kirk who ran the Girl Guides. Perfectly recognisable further back are Mr James Clark (right) and Alice Gill the sextoness (left).

The Boys' Brigade enters Chapel Lane sometime in the 1940s. The entrance to Church Farm is on the left, the wall of Old Chappelle Cottages is on the right and School House is in the centre.

Canon Edward Marshall Hall (centre, see p. 93) regularly took boys from Bishopsworth to camps in the Isle of Wight. This picture dates from the late 1930s.

Bishopsworth Girl Guides, 92nd Bristol (Bishopsworth) Company, about 1946. Back row, left to right: Shirley Whitmarsh, -?-, Patricia Kew, Pat Bracey, Sybil Sibley, Kathleen Pembury, Mildred Buckle, Pam Hall, Joan Blake, Jane Pembury. Middle row, left to right: Thelma Hollisey, Sylvie Cutting, June Poole, Joan Clare, Betty Lester (Captain), Pearl Weaver, Norah Ward, Pam Clements, Delia Bullock. Front row, left to right: Marlene Smith, -?-, Joan Bracey, Rosemary Broad, Babette Budd, Gwen Eames, Mavis Hamblin, Barbara Berry.

St Peter's Carnival, 25 June 1938, was a fancy dress extravaganza orchestrated by the wildly enthusiastic and histrionic vicar, Canon Edward Marshall Hall, to raise the final sum for the village hall in Whitchurch Lane. Actually Edwin Wyatt had paid the remaining balance of £300 but he had to be paid back. Miss Pat Childs of the 'Queen's Head' was Carnival Queen on a float passing between (right) Swiss Cottage and (left) Red House Farm cottages. Bishport Farm (Salvidge's), Whitchurch Lane, can be glimpsed centre.

The old fire tender of Bishopsworth's Fire Brigade (see p. 46) was pressed into service to transport the wild man of Borneo in a cage down St Peter's Rise. At the bottom he escaped and climbed up a tree in Manor Woods, whereupon the Fire Brigade turned a hose on him. In foreground, Mr Joe Harver and Mrs Boyce.

Left: The wild man's float was organised by the local scout group and Hubert Harris performed the key role. Right: But we cannot discover who dared to be Lady Godiva and Peeping Tom.

Left: The vicar was W.G. Grace and no doubt indulged his penchant on Highridge Common. Right: Mr Frank Owen, the church organist, was Town Crier. For 50 years he cycled miles to St Peter's from Bishopston, twice a week in all weathers. In his time the choir had sixteen trebles, six sopranos, two altos, four tenors and five basses.

Mark Simmons was born in 1907 in the tiny cottage in Whitchurch Lane next to the post office. His real Christian name was Morris but he was known as Mark. He had two brothers and five sisters: Doris, Daisy, Elsie, Maud and Ivy. He shared the back bedroom with his elder brother, Joe, whom he worshipped. Joe was killed in the First World War (see p. 68). On bath nights, two a week for girls and one for boys, water was boiled on three stoves and ladled with saucepans into a large aluminium tub before the fire. There was no main drainage, only a closet at the back over a cesspit full of cinders.

Left: Rear view of the Simmons' home. From here they moved in 1910 to Gaston Cottage which was reached by a cinder path from the Vicarage drive (now Vicarage Road). Right: Mark looks angelic enough, but he was as lively and mischievous as most village boys, often rebuked by Edwin Wyatt and Mr Moon in the choir for giggling and by Arthur Wyatt and Mr Chivers for scrumping apples and walnuts from Home Farm and the Manor House orchards.

Mark loved his mother and dad. Mr Simmons was a bricklayer and stonemason and moved from Bedminster before Mark was born. 'Dad was a good man. I never heard him swear or tell lies; he always told us to speak the truth. He suffered with deafness, but although he never went to Church he always kept the Sabbath – no work on Sundays; he used to read the Bible or a Sunday book called the Sunday Companion. Mother, on the other hand, was one who loved the Church'.

Mark became a bricklayer like his father and helped to build Headley Park, 1936-37. He spent his last years with Hilda, his wife, in a house in St Peter's Rise. Following a serious stoke c. 1976 he began writing down his memories of Bishopsworth. His story, *Mark – My Words*, was published the year before his death in 1981. This and its sequel, *Mark: More of My Words*, published 1984, are some of the most eloquent and beautiful recollections of childhood ever written. [MMW1, MMW2].

When Headley Park estate was built between 1934 and 1938, the local press went rather over the top. 'Do you know, the estate is 200 feet above sea level? What a breeze there was tonight! It sweeps over Dundry from the Mendips like – well – like the zephyr or something or other, and the scenery is fine'. Prospective buyers had the impression that it was somewhere in the wilds and had to be informed that it was only $1\frac{1}{2}$ miles from East Street.

View of Headley Park from Bedminster Down before construction began. Bottom left is the track leading from Church Road to Headley Farm. Care was taken to bend the new street round certain trees to avoid cutting them down. The bushy one in the centre survived many years at the end of Durleigh Close.

Houses were offered for sale at £360, £385 and £435. They were considered rather trendy, with small variations of design in the tile-hung bay windows and cottage-style gables. Special features included picture rails, enamelled gas stoves, and bathroom geysers 'of modern type, chromium-plated and white enamelled'. The Redcliffe Furnishing Company furnished the show-home on the estate for £45 and offered £5-worth of furniture to anyone who bought a house on the estate. The Estate Agents gave a free turkey to all new purchasers; poor Elsie Clark at Bishopsworth Post Office was inundated with turkeys!

The men who built Headley Park. The main road running through the estate was originally called 'St Michael's Rise' but was re-named 'St Peter's Rise' after the Church. [M9].

101

Whitchurch Lane, c. 1934. The 'Stony Bridge' where it crossed the Pigeon House Stream still exists, though the road is twice as wide and completely dwarfed by the dual carriageway running alongside (to the left). Today (1996) the defunct cigarette factory complex fills the left horizon, Hartcliffe Estate the right and the centre is the Hartcliffe roundabout.

Whitchurch Lane, *c.* 1940, at its junction with Novers Lane, Pigeon House Stream on the left. Pigeon House Cottages, for the use of farm labourers, marks the junction of the track (now Maynard Road, Hartcliffe) leading to Pigeon House Farm. They were demolished in 1980. Mr Tucker's bungalow in the distance, then brand new, incredibly still stands in the midst of a major road intersection and surrounded by the Hartcliffe Industrial Estate.

Left: A cloud-burst in 1931 turned the Pigeon House Stream into a raging torrent. Whitchurch Lane was flooded and people had to be rescued through the roofs of their cars. Right: It was safer to travel by horse and cart. Pigeon House Cottages at the time of the flood. At this time Mr and Mrs Beale lived in one of these cottages and next door lived their son, Alfred Beale, his wife, Hyacinth, and their five children.

Aerial photograph looking north from Dundry Hill, *c.* 1928. Whitchurch Lane runs from left to right across the middle distance. Most of the fields on the left belonged to Filwood Farm (top left); the rest belonged to Tyning Farm (top right). All this land was acquired by the city for building the new estates of Knowle West and Hartcliffe, although during the 1930s and 1940s much of it (north of Whitchurch Lane) was used for Bristol's first airport.

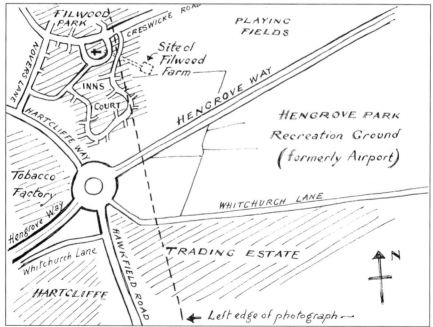

Today Hengrove Way cuts through the top of this landscape. Many fields have become recreation grounds; the land south of Whitchurch Lane is Hawkfield Business Park and Filwood Farm has disappeared under Inns Court housing estate, mostly built in the 1970s.

Looking towards Dundry Hill from Novers Lane, c. 1938. The whole of Hartcliffe now fills this landscape and this part of Novers Lane has been obliterated by the tobacco factory complex.

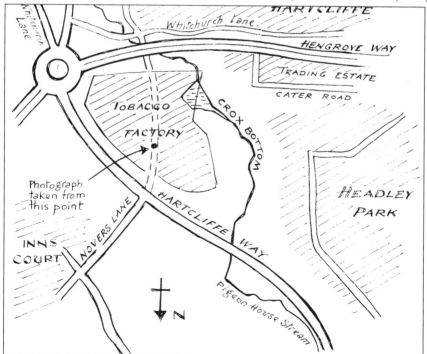

This view today would be dominated by the massive tobacco factory and administration block in the foreground and the tower blocks flanking Symes Avenue in the middle distance.

Major Roy Elton (extreme left) with visiting top brass inspecting the Bishopsworth Home Guard in Cobhorn, a field between the Church and the old Vicarage, c. 1940. The site is now the playing field of the Primary School.

Enemy flares coming down in King's Head Park, photographed by Arthur Densford in Manor Road, c. 1941. Bishopsworth lay in the flight path between the Dorset coast and the Filton aeroplane factories and suffered incendiary raids and several high explosive bombs. Four houses in St Peter's Rise were bombed flat.

Bishopsworth Home Guard did their firing practice in one of Mr Rudd's fields, Withywood Farm. Owing to the slope of the land, wooden platforms had to be erected to prevent stray bullets endangering the lives of people on Dundry Hill. Dr Wallace of the Long Ashton Research Station is firing an American Springfield (1914 vintage) and, nearest camera, Major Stokes Reece is firing a Lee-Enfield. [M10, M17].

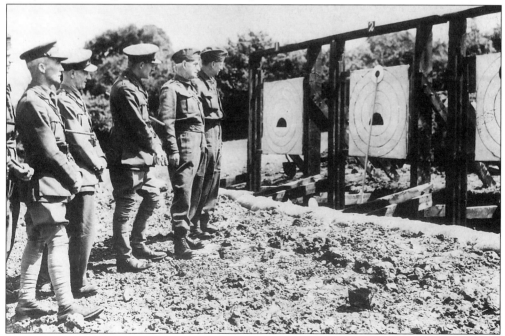

Dr Wallace (first from right) and Major Stokes Reece (third from right) examine the butts at Withywood Farm.

Warships Week in front of what was then Miss Bishop's store, March 1942. On the platform erected at the junction of Grange Road and Church Road are, from left to right: Mr W.J. Kew; Mr E.J. Iliffe JP, Chairman of the Parish Council; and the visiting naval officer, Commander Evans OBE, RN. Among the colour party are: F.O. Reakes (Home Guard), Trevor Bryant (Scouts), Beryl Chappell (Girl Guides) and Mrs Ogbourne (WVS)

From the upper window in Miss Bishop's store we get a better view of the platform party. From left to right: Major Roy Elton, Commanding Officer of Bishopsworth Home Guard; Mr E.J. Iliffe; Commander Evans and (sitting) Edwin Wyatt, Dorothy Hall, Mr Pobjoy and W.J. Kew. They were all members of the Parish Council. Further down Church Road is a Police Wolseley, and in his front garden (top centre) watching the parade, Mr Hamblin whose son Sidney was killed in the First World War (see p. 68).

SATURDAY, MARCH 21st

SPECTACULAR
FOOTBALL MATCH

FIRST AND LAST ROUND
of the
INTER——ESTING PRESENTATION CUP (?)

HOME GUARD
versus
A TEAM OF SELECTED LADIES
(Civil Defence Services)

Referee—P. C. Whitehead (with Whistle and Truncheon at the Ready).

This will be staged on the field to the rear of the School Buildings.

Kick-Off - - - 3.0.   (Every man for himself)

———::———

AND AT 7.30 P.M.

Grand Concluding
Dance

CONGREGATIONAL   HALL

ADMISSION 2/6 (4 Stamps) ————— AT DOOR
Limited to 120   7.30—11.30 p.m.
NOVELTY DANCES AND PRIZES   REFRESHMENTS

THANK YOU

BURLEIGH LTD., PRINTERS, LEWIN'S MEAD, BRISTOL.

BISHOPSWORTH'S
WARSHIP WEEK
MARCH 14th — 21st

Programme
of Events

Contains most of the interesting events that will be held and requests your complete support.

PROGRAMME   -   -   TWOPENCE

A DIARY FOR THE WEEK

A Letter from the Chairman.

Saturday, March 14th, will see the commencement of Bishopsworth's Warship Week. The goal that has been set us as part of the Long Ashton R.D.C.'s aim of £125,000 is £10,000. The Committee has prepared a series of events which I believe cover all types of local social entertainment. I ask you to give the dates your earnest attention and practical support. The country needs our small endeavours as much, if not more so than the larger and more spectacular efforts, as there are infinitely more " Bishopsworths " than, say, " Bristols."

You will notice after the various admission prices another figure in brackets, this represents the amount you will have returned to you, immediately, in National Savings Stamps.

We must not, however, lose sight of the fact, that these events constitute just the social, and, if I may say so, the advertising side of our Warship Week. The solid body of our total must be built by everybody saving and investing every penny possible. Nothing less will suffice ; nothing less will put ' Bishport ' in the headlines. Every sum, large or small, that you can invest benefits you—benefits the country—and assists us towards the position where we can say :—

BISHOPSWORTH HAS DONE IT

Go to it, and a final word in addition, keep going to it afterwards.

Thank you,
E. J. ILIFFE,
Chairman of Warship Week Committee.

SAVE AS YOU PAY TO PLAY

SATURDAY, MARCH 14th
3.0—5.30 p.m.

COMMANDER EVANS,
O.B.E., R.N.
WILL BE HERE.

A PARADE of the Home Guard, Civil Defence Services and other contingents is timed to take place this afternoon.

The Times are approximately :—

Leaves Grange	... ...	3.0
Elmtree	... ...	3.10
Highridge Common	...	3.15
King's Head Lane	...	3.35
Fire Station	... ...	3.45

Here the parade will be Inspected and a March Past with Salute has been arranged.

The Salute will be taken by
COMMANDER EVANS, O.B.E., R.N.

There will be a number of sellers of National Savings Stamps about the village this afternoon, and anyone wishing to purchase Certificates, etc., will be able to do so at either the Post Office, which will remain open until 8.0 p.m., or the Stall outside the Congregational Hall after the Parade has been dismissed.

GIVE YOURSELF A FLYING START
7.30—10.30

A SOCIAL
will be held at
THE CONGREGATIONAL HALL
BY THE BISHOPSWORTH BADMINTON CLUB
ADMISSION 1/- (2 Stamps). Refreshments at Moderate Prices

The Victory Party in Vicarage Road, 1945, took place on the site of the tennis courts in what was still part of Home Farm. The farmhouse is visible in the background and the aspect towards the south was still quite rural until the Highridge estate arrived ten years later.

Street Party, Alexandra Road. The Uplands part of Bedminster Down was less than ten years old but already a separate identity was being forged. The trees at the end were part of Home Farm, now King's Head Park.

The Victory Dinner in the Church Hall, 1945, brought all the village together with the exception of servicemen not yet demobbed. We cannot identify everyone, but on the near table are Heather Darby, Mrs Bowden and Miss Bowden. Main table, backs to wall, include: Elsie Clark, Winnie Pitman, Mrs Chandler, Mr Owen (organist), Miss Rossiter. Standing across the back are: Nellie Pitman, Miss Osmond, Mrs Plummer, Mrs Smith, George Smith, Dorothy Hall, Brian Cooper (Curate), Revd Marshall Hall, Miss Evelyn Crawford, Mrs Dobson. Backs to wall: Mary Groves, Mrs Rowatt, Will Howe, Mrs Howe, Mrs Eastman, Annie Blackmore, Mrs Jessie Clark. Inside from left towards back include: Pat Cox, Gillian Barwood and Mary Croft. Inside from right towards back: Annette Chandler, Ben Thyer, Mrs Thyer, Mr Plummer, Jack Reynolds, Mrs Reynolds, Mrs Harver, Sid Harver, Maurice Howe, Miss Woods, Miss Olive Smith, Paul Dalton (boy).

Pigeon House Farm, *c.* 1924, before it was acquired for the Hartcliffe estate. The site from which the photographer took this is now occupied by the Methodist Church in Mowcroft Road. The farm was originally called Arthur's Court and must have been part of the Manor of Bishopsworth of which the Arthurs were lords from the twelfth to the sixteenth century. The 'pigeon house', extreme left of picture, dated from the sixteenth century and undoubtedly provided the household of the Lords of the Manor with such delicacies. The other farm buildings probably date from the seventeenth and eighteenth centuries. The Malago Society possesses a facsimile copy of an interesting account book of Joseph Poole, farmer of Pigeon House Farm, for 1832 to 1838 which also records the birth of his children. In 1851 he was farming 400 acres with eleven men, which establishes Pigeon House Farm as the largest in Bishopsworth.

Bill Withers at Pigeon House Farm, *c.* 1926. His father, John Beard Withers, had been killed at Hart's Farm, near Parson Street Station, in 1906 when a train frightened his horse which threw him violently to the ground. His son, Dick, took over Hart's Farm, Bill had Pigeon House and Ernest took the nearby Pottery Farm. To the left is the sixteenth century dovecot or pigeon house which gives the farm its name.

Bill and Ernest Withers' married sister, Hepsibah, and Dorothy Russell of Church Farm, Bishopsworth. Bill and 'Hep' with their dog stand in the doorway. They retired to Tickenham c. 1950 when served with a compulsory purchase order by the city for the building of Hartcliffe.

Haymaking in Pigeon House Farm before 1914. The fields looking towards Whitchurch are now all built over. [M26].

The steeply pitched roof of Chestnut Farm in the centre of the village survives despite fairly drastic reconstruction since this photo was taken *c.* 1930. Under Harry Light and his son, Joe, it was a working farm up to the 1940s with a busy farmyard where now are front gardens. A stone in the gable of the carriage house carries the date 1607 which may be the date of the farmhouse. [M30, M31].

Left: Henry Light of Chestnut Farm was a champion sheep-shearer and judge of ploughing, thatching and hedging competitions, in which skills he was an expert. He was a member of the Loyal and Ancient Order of Shepherds and when he was buried in St Peter's churchyard in 1936 their shepherds crooks were linked over the coffin. Right: Church Farm, an attractive house with a mansard roof, stood opposite the Church on the corner of Chapel Lane and Church Road. A rank of shops replaced the farmhouse in the 1960s but its farm buildings survive as business premises (Davis Roofing Ltd).

Yew Tree Farm, approached by a track opposite the King's Head, has not appreciably altered since this photo of before 1914, although it is now dominated by the building constructed for the CEGB on Bridgwater Road in the mid-1970s (now The Pavilions).

Walter Beaton delivering milk on Gifford's Hill in the 1940s. In the background is Ostende Cottage, home of Dorothy Hall. He was born at Prospect Villa opposite and farmed at Lower Grove, Dundry, for many years. His wife died young in child-birth. He retired to a house in Perrycroft Avenue and devoted himself to country pursuits – bee-keeping, wine-making, marksmanship and horticulture. He was a fountain of knowledge about old Bishopsworth and his death in 1996 removed one of the last representatives of another age.

115

Crox Bottom Farm had belonged to the Flower family (see p. 17). The last to farm here was Mr
Vowles, seen here with his wife and son *c*. 1939. The Pigeon House Stream, controlled by a
sluice gate, drove a water mill which operated a chaff cutter. Inside the farmhouse was a huge
chimney piece which was never without a fire. A whole tree trunk was pulled through the
passageway by a pony, there being a door at each end, and the huge log was rolled into the fire.
By 1962 the farm was a ruin and today the site is obliterated by the Hartcliffe tobacco factory
complex.

Haystack fire at Pottery Farm, *c*. 1924. It was then farmed by Ernest Withers (see p. 112). When
all the other Bishopsworth farms in the Hartcliffe area were abandoned and then wrecked,
Pottery Farm, situated on what is now Grinfield Avenue, was temporarily reprieved. It became
a Scout HQ and later a probation office, but that too was demolished in the end.

Filwood Farm, 1945, the year the Halls (Anthony and family) moved to Folly Farm, Tickenham. Following compulsory purchase, the council put in a caretaker but when he was withdrawn, this 600-year old building was vandalised beyond repair and now nothing marks the site except part of the drive skirting Inns Court Estate, Knowle West.

Three hundred year old White House Farm, home to three generations of the Broad family, was evacuated in 1951. Mr Ernest Broad moved his dairy herd to Lower Wick, Dursley, and the excavators moved in to dig drains for what is the junction of Collinson Road and Randolph Avenue, Hartcliffe. The name survives in the local Primary School.

Lovelaces' shop stood opposite the Elm Tree Inn. It was a typical village emporium, supplying tobacco, cigarettes, confectionery, periodicals, ice-cream, toys and stationery. Among other invaluable services, it was Bishopsworth's first ladies hairdressing salon (upstairs), chemists and lending library. It closed in December 1966 and was demolished.

The shelf on the left displays Phensic, Anadin, Vaseline, Ex-Lax, Rennies, Hedex and Gillette razor blades. *Dandy*, *Princess* and *Rogue* feature on the magazine section to the right.

118

From the Parish Magazine, 1914. The Nelson Stores stood at the lower end of Queen's Road. It later became Honeyfield's and was a casualty of the great flood in July 1968.

From the Parish Magazine, 1942.

At the opening of the new British Legion Headquarters in Manor Road (July 1955), the Somerset standard came first, followed by the Bishopsworth standard carried by Joe Harver and with escorts, (left) Tom Cox and (right) Arnold Phillips.

The Revd Waddleton (left) came to Bishopsworth in 1954 and was the first vicar to occupy the new Vicarage in Fernsteed Road. At the opening of the British Legion Hall, W.J. Kew hands the key to Mr Norman Beese. Behind him, third from right, Mr Harry Chappell, then Mr Spratt and Mr Horace.

A function in the Congregational Church Hall. With backs to us: Mr Iliffe (in glasses), next to him Mrs Kew and W.J. Kew (half out of picture). The photographer has left his box and spare flash bulbs in a rather prominent place. Until Bishopsworth was brought inside the city of Bristol in 1951, village people paid their rates in this hall to members of the Long Ashton Rural District Council seated at a trestle table.

The Mothers' Union float in the Bishopsworth Carnival, c. 1954. Left to right: Mrs Wolfe, Janet Hill, Miss M. Hill, Mrs Parker, Mrs L.E.G. Bishop, Mrs Patch (at front), Mrs Nellie Hill.

St Peter's Bishopsworth RFC, 1937-38 season. They were regulars at the Elm Tree and played on a field behind the pub. They were allowed to call themselves 'St Peter's' on condition they occasionally went to church. From left to right, back row: ? Harris, R. Hamblin, George Tudor, Referee (?), T. Lunt, K. Bowden, E. Evans (captain), R. Mercer, S. Sullars, T. Hamblin. Front row: R. Jackson, C. Church, J. Weeks, J. Matthews, F. Perrett.

Bishopsworth United football team and some of their fans, 1947-48 season. They were affiliated to the Congregational Church and their club and changing room was at the back of the Church Hall in Grange Road. W.J. Kew supplied them with goal posts from the club he ran on Bedminster Down, and they played on Mr Gardiner's field, now the site of Fernsteed Road and Lakemead Gardens. Under the leadership of their trainer Bernard Newport (second from right) they swept all before them and in 1950 won the Gloucestershire Silver Cup at the old Bristol Rovers ground at Eastville. 7,000 fans watched the game and the Elm Tree Inn was so crowded with cheering well-wishers when they returned that they had difficulty making their way in. In those days George Sampson and Arthur Patch were the champion players.

St Peter's Easter play in the Church Hall, *c.* 1946. On the extreme right, Marjorie Read, a devoted member of the Church for many years and a keen supporter of village productions. She died in December 1994.

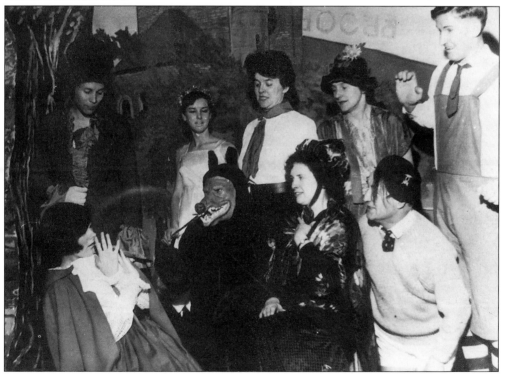

The Coronation Players flourished in the 1960s and '70s and regularly produced pantomimes in the Church Hall under the direction of Laurie Britton and Captain John Smith of the Church Army. This is *Red Riding Hood*, 1963. From left to right, back row: Anton Bantock (Dame), Mary Clare, Pat Halfyard, Norma Wyatt, Ken Wright. Front row: Ann Derrick, John Smith (Wolf), Diana Orchard, Dr Bill Sinton. Backdrop: St Peter's Church painted by John Smith.

The north wing of Bedminster Down School under construction, 1957, on the old Donald Road Recreation Ground. It was one of Bristol's four new Secondary Schools opened in 1955. The main entrance is in the centre; the new wing (left) was bonded in to the original wing.

Through the girders of the new wing can be seen the roof of the Recreation Ground pavilion, which served as a classroom for some time; and beyond that is the Gospel Hall in Donald Road.

Children assemble on the girls' playground on the opening day of the school on 8 September 1955. The photograph was taken by the newly appointed headmaster, Mr Harold Simmonds. In the background are the houses in Wraxall Grove.

The staff of Bedminster Down Secondary School, March 1957. Seated, from left to right: Mrs Bradshaw (Geography), Miss Winchester (Librarian), a Somali visiting teacher, Mr Simmonds (Headmaster), Miss Phyllis Hamer (Senior Mistress), Mr Norman Long (Deputy Head), Lt. Cdr. Naylor (Remedial Teacher). Standing, from left to right: Mr Harry Allen (Maths), Mr Arthur Spencer (History and Commerce), Mr Jerry Redmore (Geography), Mr Smyth (Head of History), Mr Brian Newman (P.E.), Mr North (French), Mr Windrum (Head of English), Mr Brian Lennox (Metal-work), Mr Walter Outhwaite (Commerce), Mr John Duncalf (Divinity), -?-, Miss Morley (Maths), Mr Cleak (Music), Mrs Worcester (Art), Miss Davies (P.E.), Miss Molly Moss (Drama), Mr Geoff Ainsley (History), Mrs Bassett (Needlework), Mr Keith Edwards (Woodwork), -?-, Mrs Miriam Morgan (Biology), -?-, Miss Yapp (Domestic Science), Mrs Dowling (Domestic Science). [M4, M19, M23].

Edwin Wyatt whose long lifespan bridges almost all the photographs in this book and who features so prominently in it, died in 1946. 1 January was his 97th birthday. He went to work as usual for the firm that he had worked for since 1864 and his employers presented him with a silver salver. 'If this salver was piled high with gold sovereigns, it would not be equal to the services Mr Wyatt has rendered to this firm,' they said. On 10 January he attended church and read the lesson, 'Arise, Shine, for thy Light is come and the Glory of the Lord is risen upon Thee'. Then he stopped. 'I can't go on,' he said. 'I can't see'. On 16 January he died. The salver engraved with the words of that last lesson was presented to the Church. [SP].

On 17 April 1956, HM Queen Elizabeth II passed through Bishopsworth on her way to open Chew Valley Lake. Dorothy Hall took this snap from her garden gate. In the distance on the left of the road is The Meade.

Princess Margaret came to Withywood in the early 1960s to open the Youth Centre in Queen's Road. She was also welcomed at St Andrew's Church, Hartcliffe.

The Great Flood, July 1968. A freak storm over Bristol turned the Malago into a raging torrent. This is St Peter's Rise under water, photographed during a flash of lightning, at the height of the storm. Pavements were ripped up, garages flattened, Honeyfield's shop at the bottom of Queen's Road devastated – but Bedminster and Ashton Gate suffered more. [M8].

LAST LOOK. – Mr and Mrs R. Tucker walk past the cottages in Chapel Road. Right: Mrs Daisy Pitman and her daughters Nellie and Winnie.

FAMILIES MOVE OUT - TO MAKE WAY FOR DEMOLITION MEN AT BISHOPSWORTH

Mr and Mrs C. Hill.

was the headline over these photographs in the *Bristol Evening World* on 6 October 1960. Ancient cottages on the village triangle, some of them going back to the chapel of ease of 1190 (see p. 18), are evacuated before demolition. Mrs Pitman and her daughter, Winnie Elverd, and Cecil Hill, who started the waggon works (see p. 80) were among those who moved to new homes. The report says: 'Of course we shall miss the old place,' said Mrs Pitman, who is sextoness of St Peter's Church, Bishopsworth. 'But in many ways, I know it will be better for us.' Mrs Pitman has had to do without 'mod cons', and rely on candle-light in the two upstairs rooms. Just round the corner, in Chapel Road, Mr and Mrs Cecil Hill were preparing to leave their cottage – after 37 years. 'I'm a bit disturbed about leaving, naturally,' said 64-year-old Wheelwright Mr. Hill, 'but the house we're going to on Highridge estate is far superior to this.' Both the Hills and Mrs Pitman will have to pay more than the few shillings rent they have been charged for their cottages, and another corner of old Bristol will disappear with hardly a murmur.